Radical Rest

Radical Rest

Rethinking Your Bucket List in the Last Days

RICHARD L. BACKES

RESOURCE *Publications* · Eugene, Oregon

RADICAL REST
Rethinking Your Bucket List in the Last Days

Resource Publications
An Imprint of Wipf and Stock Publishers
199 W. 8th Ave., Suite 3
Eugene, OR 97401

www.wipfandstock.com

PAPERBACK ISBN: 979-8-3852-1910-0
HARDCOVER ISBN: 979-8-3852-1911-7
EBOOK ISBN: 979-8-3852-1912-4

05/28/24

Contents

Introduction

The modern church is in desperate need of a revival. The "graying" of our attendees is apparent in most church bodies. Many of our children are lost to the world at an early age. Their loss is certainly no surprise when you consider the flood of nonsense and brainwashing targeting them from every direction. Parents and grandparents are often caught up in their own activities without the time or the heart to pursue dedicated and disciplined instruction of their own kids. If they have the heart and they strive to spend significant time interacting with children and grandchildren, they are often thwarted by a lack of concentration and a lack of interest on the part of the child. Let's face it, if you try to talk to them about anything other than a video game or social media, most kids' eyes glaze over immediately. You can't have a meaningful discussion when they are "plugged in" or dreaming about being plugged in.

But training a child is not all about talk, is it? It's about doing. Children emulate what they see adults do even more than what they hear adults say. But, when they are plugged in, they aren't picking up on either. Children who don't even know what their parents stand for are a part of the new reality. The mature Christian can see that society is headed off a cliff. Something needs to change.

There is a great, largely untapped source of wisdom, leadership, and available time in the modern church. This reservoir resides with the retired or nearly retired, like—perhaps—you and me. This book is dedicated to those who are approaching or currently living in retirement and are looking for insights into how they can make a difference.

I think back to the Children of Israel during the time of the judges. After God did great things for a generation of Israelites, oftentimes the very next generation started a rapid moral decline. As things worsened, the nation quickly grew weaker until they could no longer defend their own borders. The Bible often states during these periods that "every man did that which was right in his own eyes" (Judg 21:25 [ESV]). In other words, the people didn't respect the laws of God or men, and the country trended toward anarchy.

In the later stages, invaders would enter the land and subjugate the people until their lives were so miserable that they finally cried out to God. Hearing the cries, God would send a judge to lead them to victory and guide the country for a time.

Eventually, the time of the judges came to an end, and the people relinquished their sovereignty to a king. Originally, under the guidance of the law of Moses, the Israelites were supposed to follow God and his leading, but they preferred to be like every other nation around them and yield their lives, fortunes, and families to a potentially despotic leader.

I liken this Old Testament cycle to our modern moral decline. Civilization degrades to the point where Christians begin crying out to God for revival. God sends the revival which turns around a generation. But every revival generation does a poor job of transferring the joy of a changed and revived life to the next generation. The moral decline begins anew, and the cycle continues.

We would all benefit greatly if the revived generation simply placed a top priority on modeling and communicating their revived hearts and lives to the next generation!

And I have one final thought before we start. It's a thought which lends urgency as I type. Satan hates the revival cycle I just described (as imperfect as it is) and is trying to put an end to it, once and for all. He plans to change the heart of man so completely there is no memory or desire for revival. Anarchy, lawlessness, and subjugation will ensue, and people will cry out for a new leadership structure. Then he will usher in his king who will be positioned to take God's leadership role in our hearts.

Ancient Israel had tribal leadership and the cycle of judges until the people demanded a unifying central authority to replace God's system. God gave in to their demands, and they got their king. The people thought a king would concentrate the power of the nation and provide unity and strength. God warned them a king would increase their taxes, take their property, and enslave their children. God was right, of course. The new dictatorial government created division, led to moral decline, and resulted in the ultimate judgment of the nation. The kings set up their own system of worship, defied the Word of God, and preempted his authority.

In like manner, the antichrist will set himself above established governments and every moral authority. He will ride forth to conquer in the name of global unity and the greater good. Like the first king of Israel (King Saul), he will look the part of a leader. He will appear selfless, wholesome, and spiritual. Promising global peace and prosperity, he will lead the world into greater and greater decline. God's final judgment will soon follow.

However, just as Saul is a picture of the antichrist, the king who followed him is a picture of Jesus Christ!

King David was an amazing king! A man after God's own heart, he was essentially a priest, prophet, and king of Israel. From the line of David, Jesus Christ, the ultimate king, is coming to supplant the false king. It will be glorious, and I can't wait to watch things unfold!

Remember what the New Testament says about the events of the Old Testament: "Now these things happened to them as an example, but they were written down for our instruction, on whom the end of the ages has come" (1 Cor 10:11 [ESV]). God orchestrated the events of Saul's and David's lives partly so we could gain greater insights into the contrasting reigns of future world leaders.

These additional insights from the Scriptures aren't clearly spelled out as intended lessons. It is only with the near-perfect hindsight provided by the writers of the New Testament and a fundamental understanding of how amazing our God is that we see this additional content—content clearly intended for the benefit of his church. This book spends time tapping into those implied lessons and greater insights for the benefit of the retiree.

As we study from this perspective, we can also learn a lot about how detailed and intricate his plan for us is. Additionally, we must trust every jot and tittle of God's word and take the time to meditate on it.

The older generation, whose hearts still cry out for revival, must communicate God's tremendous love to those around us. We need to prepare and equip ourselves to actively resist the teachings of the world. We need to learn to spot the devices and plans of Satan while obediently standing in the gap.

This book is a call to this generation! Get your hearts right before God and begin to reach out to those around you while there is still time. You will need to find a way to unplug them first.

1

My Retirement Journey

"Trust in the Lord with all your heart, and do not rely on your own understanding. Acknowledge him in all your ways, and he will make your paths straight."

—PROV 3:5–6 (ESV)

Since retiring at age fifty, approximately twelve years ago, I have repeatedly tried to quit working—without a whole lot of success. I have tried travel, recreation, self-employment, and working with various charities. Some of these endeavors were rewarding in terms of additional income and/or a measure of fulfillment and satisfaction. But none approached the level of enjoyment I anticipated when I pulled the plug on my career.

Now, in reflection, I wonder about my decision to retire early. Why were my expectations out of sync with reality? Are they still out of sync? Did I move out of God's will for my life when I retired? How should I really look at this period of my life? Is it a time to sit back and enjoy the fruits of my many years of hard labor, or should I work just as hard as ever? These aren't questions to take lightly. My past, present, future, and even eternal rewards swirl around in

RADICAL REST

the mix and used to end up a jumbled mess in my head. At which point my thoughts would simply turn to another hobby to pursue, project to complete, or way to make money or reduce my costs. You know, typical retirement distractions.

In the midst of my struggles with retirement, my pastor announced he planned to retire in the next year or two, but he didn't want anyone to refer to his future as "retirement." He said he wanted to continue to serve in a godly ministry, and he wanted to keep his own thinking straight by calling it *repurpose-ment* instead of retirement. I liked the concept and language. In fact, I had been telling people nearly the same thing. But now, hearing the idea from someone who always said what he meant and meant what he said, the concept took on new life. I decided I needed to get serious about finishing life well!

To obtain real clarity on any subject, you must approach God's word with an open mind and a clear understanding of God's character. You can't be looking for what you want the Bible to say, because you will end up concluding the same. Religions (even Christianity) are full of the teachings of men. These deceptions are very subtle and seductive. Even good-hearted men and women who are sincerely searching God's word can fall into error.

Oftentimes, students of the Bible are looking for a unifying theory which, in their limited intellect, ties everything up into a nice bow. Or they are trying to find a compromise with the latest scientific theory. Then they will willingly change the meaning of one passage of Scripture to align with another or with science to fit their theory, because the new meaning better fits their worldview. Or they decide the Scripture that doesn't fit isn't literal or isn't specific to the situation in question.

These compromises stem from a lack of faith in the Word of God. All Scripture is God-breathed. We must understand God loves us so much he created an integrated message system literally from outside of our time domain. He carefully designed the Bible to guide us through all of life's stages and our many ups and downs. It is full of purpose, as well as irony and humor, and has many layers of meaning. If you cling to a few key verses and make them the cornerstone of your theory, then you probably are in error.

Undergirding any study must be a fundamental understanding of how good, how loving, and how faithful and true the God of the universe is. He does not lord over you as a slave-master. He is not an angry, vindictive God. He always acts in love and goodness, and he guides your life and your actions for both your own good and his glory. He understands your strengths, your weaknesses, and the desires of your heart. He knows what will make you feel fulfilled or will leave you lacking.

At the same time, he holds your eternity in his hands and already knows the glorious rewards he wants to share with you when your time on earth ends.

Before we venture into the heart of the Scriptures and issues regarding retirement, let's make sure we are on the same page.

2

Drop the Bucket before
You Kick the Bucket

"You adulterous people! Do you not know that friendship with the world in enmity with God? Therefore whoever wishes to be a friend of the world makes himself an enemy of God."

—Jas 4:4 (ESV)

When you are old enough to approach retirement issues, your thoughts and thought processes are nearly set in concrete. The longer our thoughts follow these channels, the less awareness we have that we operate from a set of preconceived ideas.

Don't get me wrong. Not having to think through concepts from scratch every time the gray matter starts churning is handy. On the other hand, pre-conceptions can make it difficult for an author to stay on the same page as his readers.

So, before we discuss the period we commonly call "retirement," let's make sure we agree on pertinent issues. As we should when sorting through any concept, let's start our discussion at the beginning. In fact, if you would indulge me briefly, let me take you back to the very beginning of men and women on earth.

Adam and Eve lived in paradise. They frolicked, played, and worked in a perfect garden setting. God himself visited often and treated them as friends. They had no concern for food, clothing, houses, or possessions. God and the garden he created provided everything. Stress, pressure to perform, and consideration for getting ahead had no place in the garden or its inhabitants. In fact, there wasn't even a well-developed concept of "mine" versus "yours," as they had everything in common. Therefore, neither competition nor strife existed in the beginning.

But temptation arose, and Eve was fooled by Satan. Adam wasn't fooled, but his was the ultimate responsibility for complying with God's direction not to eat the fruit. So, they both fell. God mercifully spared them but ejected them from the garden of Eden which they had so enjoyed. He sent them out into the world where they were to be introduced to a plethora of concepts which had likely never entered their heads. Like the comedian who used to say, "Here's your sign," God had an angel chase them out and, in essence, said, "Here's your bucket." Now, before I explain what I mean by the word "bucket," let me say I don't mean to call God flippant or uncaring. He was sadly aware of the consequences they would receive because they had put their own thoughts and desires above his direction.

I don't know where the concept of life as carrying a bucket originated, but it is common in everyday expressions and old songs. Most people who have thought about it picture a bucket holding all their money and worldly possessions. They would probably think of their life as a bucket with a hole in it; no matter how they try to fill it up, everything keeps slowly leaking out. They might find a way to fill it faster and get ahead for a while, but the fuller the bucket gets, the faster everything leaks out of the hole!

I really can relate to the bucket concept but would not limit the bucket to carrying just our money and possessions. I see it as also holding our self-image, based on our perceived status and accomplishments. I include our education and degrees, our family prestige, and our position in the community including our past and present work history, among other things.

At this point I am not addressing whether these are bad things in general. I am simply stating that our tendency to accumulate all of these things and regard them pridefully originated when sin blossomed in the garden and then took root as Adam and Eve's descendants began to cope with life out in the big, cold world.

When they left the garden and settled down in the wide world, they probably didn't realize what lay ahead. They likely didn't even understand the concept of "mine" yet. Little children say, "Mine, mine, mine" when they refuse to share their toys or candy, but Adam and Eve were more innocent than children. In the garden, they had all they wanted, and they had it in common. They did not need to compete over resources. They had no concept of saving up nor fear of losing what they had saved.

Surprisingly, God wasn't content with merely handing them their buckets and booting them out of the garden! He took their buckets and poked some big holes in them! He said things like, "Cursed is the ground because of you . . . thorns and thistles, it shall bring forth for you" (Gen 3:17 [ESV]). *Poke.* And he said, "For you are dust and to dust you shall return" (Gen 3:19 [ESV]). Roughly translated for my descriptive purpose, God says, "You will lose the battle to fill your bucket. Eventually, the last bit will drain out of the bottom as you return to the dust from which you came."

Ever since that time, men and women everywhere have striven against nature and each other to fill their buckets. They love to compare the level in their buckets to their neighbors'. They love to talk about and display everything in their buckets. They get excited about increasing the flow rates into their buckets, and some people even get excited about trying to plug some of the holes (yes, I am speaking fondly about you fellow retirees who switch coffee shops to save a nickel).

To fill their buckets, people look for things which look good to the eye, things to fill the senses, and things to elevate themselves over others, such as increased knowledge or supposed wisdom. And they love to showcase these things to other people so they can improve their self-image, that is, fill their buckets. Of course, these are the very reasons Eve decided to start us down this road by eating the fruit. Genesis 3:6 says, "So when the woman saw that the tree was good for food, and that it was a delight to the eyes, and that the tree was to be desired to make one wise, she took of its fruit and ate, and she also gave some to her husband" (ESV). By desiring these things more than desiring to obey God and enjoy his fellowship forever, Adam and Eve chose the broad path of destruction and earned their buckets! The same choice faces every person in every stage of life.

God, a wonderful, warm, and loving Father, didn't point out their buckets with relish or glee. Like a good earthly father, he let the couple make their decisions and then made them live with the consequences. However, he also devised a plan—an alternative to the bucket. His plan would take thousands of years to bring to fruition, but some of the benefits were immediately available to the pair.

Even as they picked up their buckets for the first time, he told them a child of the woman would someday crush the head of the serpent. The book of Genesis includes only this snippet of their conversation at the time. I think it is likely he told them more about the coming Messiah, though, because shortly thereafter we find Abel bringing an acceptable sacrifice of the firstborn of his flock—a sacrifice which pointed forward to the Lamb of God who takes away the sins of the world.

Unfortunately, many people who have heard about the Messiah have seen him as a nice addition to their buckets. In the Old Testament times, the Jews thought having the Law and the Prophets made them special and set them above the heathens around them. In the church era, many people believe calling themselves a Christian makes them sound like a good person. In their minds, they put a nice shiny cross in their buckets and then go on with their worldly ways without a changed life.

Or, possibly even worse, many people have seen Jesus as a way to fill up their buckets with other things. Today, prosperity preachers tell you Jesus will give you the job, the home, or the car you've always wanted. They see a full bucket as a reflection of God's favor and approval on your life. They will probably tell you to send them a seed offering so God can bless you and increase the flow rate into your bucket. These prosperity preachers aren't new, and they aren't selling you a new concept. They merely fill a demand which people have had ever since God said, "Here's your bucket." Once you are aware of it, you see this demand present throughout history!

The ancient Israelites who worshiped Jehovah *and* the gods of the pagans around them simply hedged their bets against angry pagan gods who wanted to poke more holes in their buckets. If you believe in the possible existence of multiple gods who might be vengeful and petty, logically you will spread your worship and time around in an effort to appease them all, thus "preventing" the cursing of your crops or your family.

The followers of Jesus when he walked this earth also lacked clarity on the concept. When Jesus fed the five thousand, they immediately wanted to make him king by force. Jesus understood they wanted to make him king because they finally had found someone who could fill their buckets! As he explained later, they didn't understand or want what he offered. Either they desired to add him to their buckets so they could be more "spiritual" than their friends and neighbors, or they were simply eager to have him fill their buckets with worldly provisions.

I think many so-called Christians today are in the same boat with the five thousand. However, Jesus doesn't have a plan to make you wealthy or to make your life easier. Instead, he offers a completely different option to the bucket! What is the option, you ask? Well, I will gladly tell you more in the next chapter, but first, you must come to the realization that no matter what you think about Christianity or what *anyone* has told you, Jesus does not plan to simply fill your bucket!

You might wonder what these buckets have to do with retirement. Well, the path the one and only Savior of the world has called you to is a radical path. It's a narrow trail through a solitary gate. To successfully navigate this path, you need to be looking forward and up. You can't be looking back at your old life or down at your bucket. The last steps along the narrow path have some unique features and pitfalls. God will hold your hand at times and he will carry you at others. A rusty old bucket will inhibit both!

3

A Tale of Two Buckets

"Looking to Jesus, the founder and perfecter of our faith, who for the joy that was set before him endured the cross, despising the shame, and is seated at the right hand of the throne of God."

—HEB 12:2 (ESV)

As I started to research the subject of retirement and saw the concept of humans toting buckets through life, I struggled to discern a suitable replacement for the bucket. I first thought of how Jesus wants us to put down our buckets and pick up the cross. Of course, the mandate is scriptural, but it doesn't communicate to most people the concepts they need to move successfully through the retirement transition.

When people think about picking up their cross and following Jesus, they visualize a slow, agonizing journey. The Via Dolorosa was possibly the most agonizing walk ever known, filled with the fog of pain, the torture of humiliation, separation from the presence of the Father, and grief for the sins of the world. It's a heavy lift to get modern-day retirees to put down the buckets they have spent much of their lives filling, polishing, and prepping for retirement, and simply pick up an old rugged cross. Who wants to remove their crown of life's accomplishments and put on a circle of thorns?

Yet, didn't Jesus do this very thing? Taking no thought for himself, he strove to do the Father's will, sacrificing himself for your sins and mine. Certainly, we must emulate our Lord Jesus, and, in this book, I can deliver no different message.

But then it struck me! Jesus *was* carrying a bucket even during the final walk to Golgotha's hill. The bucket so differed from our earthly buckets that it simply wasn't recognizable to my human sensibilities. The author of Hebrews wrote in chapter 12 verse 2, "[Jesus] for the joy that was set before him endured the cross, despising the shame, and is seated at the right hand of the throne of God" (ESV).

So, Jesus looked forward to his eternal rewards while he endured the cross! He carried a golden bucket of sorts. Unlike our holey old tin buckets, his bucket and its contents were sound and incorruptible.

Notice, the text doesn't read "*rewards* set before him" but "*joy* set before him." The word "joy" includes more than rewards. Joy came from knowing a return to heaven was imminent. Soon he would sit down beside the Father on the throne. He would be reunited with men and women whom he had known on earth but who had passed, like probably his earthly father, Joseph. Joy emanated from the knowledge of the love, joy, and fellowship he would generate in the hearts of his followers through the succeeding centuries and his ultimate reunion with all of those disciples.

Plus, Jesus was looking forward to giving gifts and eternal rewards to those who would follow as his disciples. The ultimate concern for another person regards their eternal welfare. This concern starts with an urgent desire to witness to them and includes heartfelt prayers for salvation, but it doesn't stop there.

Jesus said, "Whatever you bind on Earth will be bound in Heaven, and whatever you loose on Earth will be loosed in Heaven" (Matt 18:18 [NIV]). I have heard different theories about what this means. At the very least, it implies we should pray about eternity. I therefore believe praying for someone else should include praying about their eternal rewards as well as their eternal destiny.

I know praying for someone else's eternal rewards sounds presumptuous, but God loves when we pray about things which really matter. Praying for eternal rewards shows we understand and share a little of his eternal perspective.

I have frequently prayed such a prayer for my wife. She has what they used to call a "tin ear," meaning she has no ear for music whatsoever (she has mixed feelings about my sharing this). For many years she refused to sing at all in church, but I have encouraged her to make a joyful noise anyway. In the last few years, she has started to try. It is so sweet and encouraging to hear her soft but slightly discordant notes! It's a joy to the Lord and to myself. (I'm not sure about the folks around us, though.) By trying to sing, she shows that praising and glorifying God is more important to her than what the people who listen might think of her!

My prayer for her is for God to reward her with a sweet singing voice in heaven. I know this specific prayer is way above my pay grade! However, it's selfless and loving. Plus, it shows proper priorities and a focus on eternity—the kind of prayer God longs to hear from his children.

I also pray missionaries I know will dedicate themselves to God's service in a selfless manner and win many to Christ so their rewards will be great in heaven.

Ultimately, I know his is "the kingdom and the power and the glory" (Matt 6:13 [NKJV]), and I don't know how exactly he will hand out rewards. Still, as we emulate our Lord and Savior, these are the sorts of things we should carry in our hearts, looking forward to the joy set before us!

So then let's resume setting the stage concerning Jesus' carrying a golden bucket to the cross.

I believe what Adam and Eve did in the garden changed humanity on earth forever. The Tree of the Knowledge of Good and Evil transformed the thinking of man. The concept of a bucket was introduced there and will never depart from our psyche this side of heaven. The fall introduced self-awareness and made the desire to work toward our own future and benefit a reality. As a result, God knew that people on earth would always carry a bucket.

In fact, when Satan said to Adam and Eve in Gen 3:5, "For God doth know that in the day ye eat thereof, then your eyes shall be opened, and ye shall be as gods, knowing good and evil" (KJV), he knew that this was at best a half-truth (he is a liar and the father of lies). However, the lie was also a curious distortion of what really happened.

Instead of making them like gods, the sin in the garden ultimately made God more like man. God the Father sent the Son to be born like us and to live and die like us. He received a glorious new body and entered into the presence of the Father where, I believe, he will retain an essence of humanity (not to mention the scars he received from us) forever.

Satan portrayed sin's results so backwards, didn't he? Instead of evilly desiring to withhold godhood from man, God was willing to take on the form of a man and die in our place to save us from the consequences of eating the fruit.

Tempted but without sin, Jesus, like all of us, bore the bucket of self-awareness and a desire to live for a better future. But rather than seeking the path of short-term and limited earthly resources and rewards, Jesus took the long view. The long view led him down a short road carrying a heavy, rugged cross. He willingly endured even that for the glorious rewards he carried in his flawless bucket.

So, it's simply not a biblical teaching to just drop your bucket. Pandora's box has been opened. As long as we remain on earth, humans will never be the same as Adam and Eve in the garden. Even Jesus Christ, our perfect example of a perfect life, carried his own bucket, albeit a bucket of a different sort.

We ought to be realists about working for eternal rewards. I have done Bible studies with men who all agreed they didn't care about eternal rewards. They just wanted to follow Jesus here on earth with all their hearts.

I understood and struggled to argue the point with them, but their stance didn't strike me as completely realistic. When Jesus carried the cross and the Father temporarily abandoned him, the thought of eternal joys carried him through. In fact, Jesus himself said in Matt 6:20, "But lay up for yourselves treasures in heaven, where neither moth nor rust destroys and where thieves do not break in and steal" (ESV). Here Jesus himself directs us to abandon our leaky buckets and seek eternal treasures.

So, Jesus knows we all carry a bucket. It's been the nature of man ever since the fall to do so. The question is which bucket will we carry. Which are you carrying right now? Are you still toting a leaky bucket half full of rusty, moth-eaten junk, or have you traded it in for the flawless bucket Jesus carried to the cross?

I think most of us convince ourselves we are working for the Kingdom of God, but we have never put down our rusty human treasures. Trust me when I say you can't do both. A man can't carry two buckets at once; you can't serve money and God simultaneously (Matt 6:24, paraphrased).

Luke wrote in chapter 12 of his gospel, "Where your treasure is, there will your heart be also" (v 34 [ESV]). Elsewhere Scripture describes a double minded man as unstable in all his ways (Jas 1:8 [KJV]). This statement is true because neither God nor man can trust a person holding two buckets to strive to fill the right one. You never know his motivation to do the things he does.

Don't attempt to carry two buckets. Work out your salvation with the fear and trembling it deserves (Phil 2:12, paraphrased). If you suspect you are still toting an old bucket around, come with me on this journey, and we will take a closer look.

4

Examine Your Bucket

"Oh Lord, you have searched me and known me! You know when I sit down and when I rise up; you discern my thoughts from afar. You search out my path and my lying down and are acquainted with all my ways. Even before a word is on my tongue, behold, O Lord, you know it altogether."

—Ps 139:1–5 (ESV)

If you are anything like me, you have spent your Christian life struggling to put down your bucket completely. If you want to complete the journey, you must examine yourself for unneeded burdens you are still dragging around. However, some critical heart issues make the examination difficult and must be dealt with first.

I have been a Christian since I was six years old. I have worked hard to get ahead and save money for retirement. I married a Christian woman. With God's constant help, we raised three fine children, and we hope to continue to impact the lives of our family. In general, we understand what God wants in our lives, and we (usually) yield to his direction.

But, as I examined my retirement, I felt I was lacking focus. There was a general malaise attached to the whole retirement issue. Certainly, I wanted to finish strong, but I felt far from the goal. I lacked something in my focus and purpose.

Before I could make any progress in this area, I needed to come to grips with my own mindset. After going in circles for a while, I realized this was a job for God! I had spent a lifetime creating the mindset I had! I had scraped and saved and planned for years, and then I counted down the days (literally marking them off a calendar) until retirement. Prolonged, emotionally intense thought patterns like this create deeply worn channels in the old brain.

Plus, as we become "more mature," we struggle more to admit to ourselves we don't really have a clue! In other words, the more time, energy, and thought we put into our retirement plans, the more vested and defensive we become.

A couple of years ago, if you had asked me how I was enjoying retirement, I would have given the normal platitudes about staying busy but not having a boss (except my wife). I would have gently bragged about our travels and leisure activities. The subtle implications in my answer would have hinted my wife and I were hard-working, organized, relatively wealthy, smart, and capable. All good American Christians plan and save all their lives, right? Then they implement their retirement plan and take pictures of themselves out traveling, fishing, or golfing and post those on social media so their families, ex-coworkers, and fellow retirees can see how they have their act together.

I have been asking God to help me work through these issues for him and to refocus and repurpose me to finish well. He has been gracious beyond measure. Let me share a few things he has pointed out in my own life.

First, he has gently pointed out that retirement is a radical change. You probably know people who have retired from work only to become sick and/or die shortly thereafter. Retirement absolutely shocks your system! It doesn't seem logical, does it? Stress should be gone, and life should suddenly be a lot easier. It often doesn't work this way, however. Without a job, many people (especially guys, I believe) feel like they have lost their identity. After spending their adult life building their income and their career—including, perhaps, their power and authority—suddenly they feel like they are just another unemployed old has-been. Western cultures, where age and experience don't have an intrinsic value and the wisdom of the aged is seldom sought out by others, provide the perfect atmosphere for retirees to feel obsolete.

This sets up a curious tension. God doesn't want the aged to demand respect or to browbeat the young into deference. They shouldn't have to. On the other hand, youth should not ignore the wisdom of folks who have already been around the block a time or two. We would be smart to teach our young to value this wisdom and to seek it out. How great a sadness to see so many of our elderly sitting in nursing homes, unappreciated and unvisited, their wisdom squandered by those who need it most.

This feeling of obsolescence contributes to how retirement shocks our system. If the bucket represents our concept of self, oftentimes a person's biggest, brightest item in the bucket is his or her job. Retirement involves the loss of that so you can see why the retiree may feel depressed. Think of how people who lost jobs, businesses, and personal fortunes during the Great Depression threw themselves out of windows and jumped off buildings.

The typical person doesn't understand any of this during the last days at the job. We think it will be easy to adjust to a more leisurely lifestyle. As retirement draws near, we strive to convince ourselves work is becoming more trouble than it is worth and we would be better off without it. At the time, we don't really understand our buckets, nor do we fully comprehend that the job is the shiniest thing in the bucket.

What happens when we receive a shock to our identities like this? In the flesh, we compensate. We dig through our old rusty buckets, inspecting and admiring each item. We spend a lot of time comparing ours to what other folks carry in theirs. We dig out our old trophies, polishing and displaying them for the world to admire. We may showcase our leisure time, world travels, degrees and education, charity efforts, work accomplishments, and possessions. We don't want to brag directly, so we find ways to do it subtly. We just want others to envy our life choices and our lifestyle.

In short, we reinforce our own self-image and feed our pride. Then we justify our lifestyle choices by telling ourselves we have worked hard to get where we are and deserve this time to enjoy life.

Don't get me wrong. I *am not* saying you can't enjoy this period of your life. But you, like me, might be focused on the wrong things for the wrong reasons.

5

Things that Keep Us from Examining Our Buckets: Pride

"Why do you see the speck that is in your brother's eye, but do not notice the log that is in your own eye?"

—MATT 7:3 (ESV)

Pride prevents you from examining your earthly bucket! Pride is like the log in the eye that Jesus mentioned in Luke 6:42: "You hypocrite, first take the log out of your own eye, and then you will see clearly to take out the speck that is in your brother's eye" (ESV). You can't examine the contents of your bucket with a big stick in your eye!

Early in my retirement, God dealt with me pretty strongly in this area. Pride still rears its ugly head more frequently than I would like to admit, but he has guided me through, eliminating what I hope is the majority of it.

He has shown me that he so wants to perfect the hearts of his children. Jesus prays and intercedes for us every day so we will be conformed to his image. He has a plan to reach that goal. He has given us all the tools we need to change the way we think and to overcome the roadblocks Satan and society put in our path.

There are so many Bible verses against pride I can't begin to cover them all. Let me give you a few of my favorites:

- Prov 16:18: "Pride goes before destruction, and a haughty spirit before a fall." (ESV)

- Prov 29:23: "A man's pride will bring him low, but the humble in spirit will retain honor." (ESV)

- Dan 4:37: "Now I Nebuchadnezzar, praise and extol and honor the King of heaven, all of whose works are truth, and his ways justice. All of those who walk in pride he is able to put down." (ESV)

- 1 John 2:16: "For all that is in the world—the lust of the flesh and the lust of the eyes and the pride of life—is not of the Father, but is of the world." (ESV)

Pride comes in so many forms you might not always recognize it. If you have ever made a serious attempt to recognize pride and deal with it, you have discovered it grows layer upon layer in your heart and mind. I have often dealt with the surface layer only to find out the vast bulk lurks beneath the surface, much like an iceberg. If you were to cut off the exposed part of an iceberg, five percent of the remaining ice would surface.

But unlike ice, once identified, pride can't just be removed. It shrinks under the microscope of self-examination and then crops up somewhere else, usually in a more sinister and harder-to-detect form.

Thus, pride can only truly be eliminated when it is replaced with humility. Humility comes when we quit comparing ourselves with others and start to compare ourselves to God: his power, his attributes, and his standards for us. But before we can effectively do this, we have to understand who he is and what those standards are! So, the best recipe for dealing with pride is to:

1. Stay immersed in your Bible.

2. Pray daily for the Holy Spirit to help you replace pride with humility.

3. Get out in the world; serve and interact with others in a lowly and humble manner.

This process will likely take years unless you approach it seriously. And the higher your position in the workforce and the greater your standing in the community prior to retirement, the longer it might take.

Yet God has all the power and all the time he needs to do the job, and he knows exactly where you are lacking. He wants you to finish well. So, take heart; God will work powerfully to see this through!

So, if you project the image of an important man or woman, due in part to the past jobs you've had, get rid of the shiny monument to yourself that weighs your bucket down. Remember, God gave you the job you had as a temporary provision for you and your family. Ask God to give you a meek and humble heart. Remember Moses, who walked with God and led millions of Israelites. According to Numbers, he was the meekest man on earth!

6

Things That Keep Us from Examining Our Buckets: Bitterness

"See to it that no one fails to obtain the grace of God that no 'root of bitterness' springs up and causes trouble, and by it many become defiled."

—HEB 12:15 (ESV)

Like pride, bitterness can cloud your vision, making it impossible to clearly see the contents of your bucket. It's like a log sticking out of your other eye! Bitterness is almost as insidious as pride. It's hard to detect because you see the world through this bad lens every day. The distorted vision actively and continuously reinforces your distorted concept of the world.

Retirees usually deal with a certain amount of bitterness from their years on the job. Maybe the job never fulfilled you, maybe your employer never valued your contributions, or maybe you fell victim to office politics. Or it could have been one of a hundred other things that caused you to leave the employment world less than satisfied.

Perhaps to you, the work you did and the positions you held felt more like indentured servanthood or even slavery. You likely carry bitterness, hidden or otherwise. In my mind, bitterness is synonymous with unforgiveness.

The issue of bitterness is just as serious as the issue of pride. It needs to be dealt with immediately.

God chose to address the issue of bitterness and unforgiveness in my life as well. I must admit I held some bitterness about a couple of incidents during my career. I asked God to help me forgive, and together we dealt with it to an extent. But, over the years, I found myself thinking about what happened and a strong curiosity remained about what went on behind the scenes. Who had done what to me, why did they do it, and did they feel justified? I really wanted to find out so I could "put my curiosity to rest." I didn't feel particularly angry or vengeful, just curious.

I had stayed in contact with some of those involved and was dying to delve into the details with them, but I knew to do so would mean picking at scabs and feeling uncomfortable. Then I heard a wise preacher say that if you believe you were an injured party in some situation and it has driven deep, maybe unseen, roots of bitterness, you will feel a strong need to find out who did what to you and why. He explained that this is because bitterness stems from the belief you have been wronged and the other party owes you. This is a debt you intend to collect some day in some way. But first, you must determine who was responsible and if their actions were personal and malicious. You are simply trying to find out how much they owe before you collect!

Wow, I realized bitterness can be as insidious and deceitful as pride! I hadn't fully eliminated my bitterness. I simply decided to postpone my revenge until I knew more. I didn't feel anger or have a strong need for revenge, but a smoldering root remained, ready to metastasize once I knew the full truth. So, praying about it and then sticking it on the back burner is no way to fully address bitterness! I think with God's help you can deal with it through three simple guidelines:

1. Maintain a sense of humor toward yourself. Don't take yourself too seriously.

2. Trust God will judge the guilty parties for whatever they did.

3. Realize they make mistakes just like you.

Eventually, I could chuckle remembering the situations that had occurred and say to myself, "Maybe I deserved it. I will let God worry about the details." I don't need to relive the past or know more about what happened. I am not in charge of keeping the books on their life details.

The words of Exod 15:22–27 helped me release my bitterness. Just after the Children of Israel left four hundred years of slavery in Egypt and struck out from the Red Sea area, they came across a well called Marah. They were desperate for water, as they had been walking in the wilderness for three days. They tasted the well only to discover it was bitter. They murmured and complained, as was their tendency, and God interceded for them. He instructed Moses to throw a certain log into the well and the water turned sweet.

Regarding this incident, God says in verse 26, "'If you will diligently listen to the voice of the Lord your God, and do that which is right in his eyes, and give ear to his commandments and keep all his statutes, I will put none of the diseases on you that I put on the Egyptians, for I am the Lord, your healer'" (ESV). The Lord your healer is "Jehovah Rapha," which means the Lord who continues to heal, the Lord who thoroughly and completely makes whole, or the Lord who mends and repairs completely. God purified the bitter waters and his immediate comments focused on healing his children!

This is a passage in which God provided layers of meaning in his word, layers which take a little thought and meditation to fully digest. So, let's delve a little deeper.

Despite what some Bible commentators might say about the log, the act wasn't merely the gift of knowledge at work! God didn't show Moses a log that had the correct chemicals to counteract the bitterness of the water. Rather, God performed a miracle and gave us an important picture of Jesus' miraculous work on the cross.

By this miracle, he showed us that the old, rugged log of the cross, thrown by God into the waters of humanity, can completely and miraculously purify those waters! Four hundred years of slavery can create intense bitterness, but even that bitterness is no match for God! On a personal level, he also shows that the blood of Jesus, dropped in the well of your soul, can totally purify your heart and mind!

The entire journey from Egypt is a series of pictures and lessons for the Children of Israel, the church of today, and you and me on a personal level. For instance, we know leaving Egypt and crossing the Red Sea symbolizes leaving the land of sin and death (Egypt) and crossing the Red Sea (red for a reminder of Christ's blood!) through the miraculous intervention of God and his provision of a Savior (Moses was a picture of Jesus). Likewise, the well of Marah symbolizes the bitterness in our hearts.

Like the bitter waters in the heart of the well needed to be addressed, God was showing them (and us) that after salvation they (and we) must immediately confront any bitterness and unforgiveness in our hearts.

In case you think I am reading too much into this occasion, let me review what God said to the Israelites at the well with the knowledge that these things happened to them as an example to us. We read in Exod 15, ". . . and the water became sweet. There the Lord made for them a statute and a rule, and there he tested them, saying, 'If you will diligently listen to the voice of the Lord your God, and do that which is right in his eyes, and give ear to his commandments and keep all his statutes, I will put none of the diseases on you that I put on the Egyptians, for I am the LORD, your healer'" (ESV). Remember, the name of God referred to in this passage is Jehovah Rapha, which means God who continuously preserves, heals, and perfects.

God shows us here what the cross can do in our hearts, and then he confirms it by declaring himself our healer, our purifier, and our perfecter! He gently reminded the Children of Israel of his status as judge of their captors. He had judged the Egyptians through the plagues and other diseases he put on them. So, in essence, God said, "Leave their judgment to me, and I will spare you from a similar fate."

Unforgiveness and thoughts of retribution act like acid in your very soul. They slowly devour the person who carries them, while the ones who triggered the bitterness to start with are often oblivious. But forgiving others is not something that comes from a formula or can come by human wisdom or earthly counsel. It comes only by the healing power of God!

Forgiveness is required of the Christian, in part because we *must* acknowledge God has forgiven us of a much greater debt. Only a hypocrite can accept God's forgiveness as a gift, while demanding a pound of flesh from a fellow sinner as payment for a much smaller debt.

Look at what Jesus endured at the hands of men! He bears marks on his eternal body which will forever proclaim the unjustified and reprehensible treatment men showed their creator. But do you think he still dwells on what Pilate did or sits around gnashing his teeth about how the soldiers treated him on the day of his crucifixion? To the contrary, he dealt with the issue immediately and even said, "Father, please forgive them for they know not what they do."

Oh, if only we could learn to confront unforgiveness immediately and not allow it to fester! Paul wrote, "Don't let the sun go down on your wrath" (Eph 4:26 [ESV]). He assures us the Holy Spirit will purify our hearts through Jesus' saving work on the cross. But notice: the promise to heal us of bitterness and continue to perfect us is a conditional one. Here in Exodus, he says we must diligently listen to his voice and do what is right in *God's* eyes, not our own. Then he will cleanse our bitterness and protect us from the plagues and diseases of Egypt to boot!

Jehovah Rapha is waiting! He is the living and sweet water that will never leak from your golden bucket! Drink from the water he provides, and you will never thirst again. Take the bitterness that distorts your vision and give it all to him. After salvation, releasing your bitterness is one of the first steps to leaving your old rusty bucket behind!

In addition to bitterness toward coworkers and supervisors, many other forms of bitterness and unforgiveness can plague us. Bitterness toward God, family, and even ourselves manifest throughout our lives. When examining your heart during retirement, consider the bitterness you carry toward yourself, stemming from how you conducted yourself through your working years in terms of honesty, integrity, and work ethic. Then, ask God to forgive you for your behavior and your lack of forgiveness towards yourself.

A lot of us have a fundamental misunderstanding of how to ask God for forgiveness. You can't just pray, confess, and beg for mercy until you think God is at least partly appeased. You must pray in faith until you "pray through," meaning you must pray until God replaces your unbelief with a calm assurance and a joy in knowing your sins are forgiven. Ask yourself, "Do I know if I died today God would receive me into heaven and this sin wouldn't be an issue?" You must leave the throne room understanding you are justified and cleansed by his blood. Your fellowship *must* be restored so you have no barriers to communication with God and no residual anger or unsettled issues.

If you fail to pray through, a barrier will remain between you and God but little or no barrier between you and your sin! It will be too easy to fall back into sin if you think it still separates you from God.

This feeling of separation is like the old man joke I sometimes tell: you know you are old when you bend over to tie your shoe and you look around to see if there's something else you can do while you are down there! If you feel like you are separated from God anyway, you might as well soak up a few more of the pleasures of sin while you are down at its level. What do you have to lose? You tell yourself you will get fully restored someday!

Pride and bitterness block our vision tremendously. Put simply, we engage our pride to make our own buckets appear fuller (to us) than they are. In a similar manner, our bitterness makes other people's buckets appear less full to us. Remember, in a fallen world, bucket levels are all about comparisons.

7

Worldly Ideas

"See to it that no one takes you captive by philosophy and empty deceit, according to human tradition, according to the elemental spirits of the world, and not according to Christ."

—Col 2:8 (ESV)

If you have been in the workplace for twenty or thirty years (or more!), you are likely carrying a sort of residual mental fog. It comes from being saturated with the thoughts and ideas of a worldly system and the sinful people who populate it. This saturation creates a hazy film that keeps us from seeing clearly. Even with pride and bitterness removed, we can't examine the contents of our buckets with these ideas clouding our vision.

An endless number of worldly concepts may have penetrated your subconscious through the influence of your employers and peers. Think of the occasion when Jesus healed a blind man. After the healing, Jesus asked if he could see. In Mark 8:24–25 we read, "He looked up and said, 'I see people; they look like trees walking around.' Once more Jesus put his hands on the man's eyes. Then his eyes were opened, his sight was restored, and he saw everything clearly" (NIV). A two-stage miracle like this only occurs once in the Bible. In it, Jesus engages with the blind man in sort of a bio-feedback loop to fine-tune the healing.

Obviously, Jesus has unlimited power, and he didn't need to heal the man this way. Jesus performed the healing in this manner as a lesson to us, and the miracle provides the perfect illustration of the concept that sometimes healing must come in steps. Often these phases require some introspection and reflection on our part, along with an ongoing dialog with God. This is especially true with issues involving how we see the world since our vision is altered by preconceived ideas and deeply channeled patterns of thought we are largely unaware of!

After God has moved mightily to clear the logs of pride and bitterness out of the retirees' eyes so they can function normally, God still has work to do in us. He will need to rid us of the worldly thoughts and concepts which limit the examination of our buckets.

Removing these requires a miraculous intervention, but you need to be engaged in the process by searching your soul and identifying the issues one by one. Engineers call such a process "iterating to a solution." In other words, tackle the big things first. Doing so gets you in the general neighborhood of a solution. Then you re-examine the factors and fine-tune the calculation. You may need to repeat the process several times before you arrive at the correct answer.

These worldly ideas are often thoughts and concepts we take for granted; they are pre-wired (so to speak) into our thought processes but are fundamentally flawed. In our later years, we feel unable to identify and then change these concepts we have held for a large portion of a lifetime. But again, God calls us to be overcomers. He will help us because he knows these things can only be accomplished by the hand of Jesus combined with a willing and obedient heart!

Here are a few examples of these haze-inducing false concepts:

FALSE CONCEPT #1: GOD HELPS THOSE WHO HELP OTHERS

Many people (and even Christians) believe a deceptive phrase: "cast your bread on the waters." It started out as a biblical reference, and you will hear some people say it whenever they see something nice done for others. We find the full text in Eccl 11:1: "Cast your bread on the waters: for you will find it after many days" (ESV). The verse expresses a general concept that if you are generous to others, they will tend to be generous to you someday. It has the same meaning as another common phrase: "What goes around comes around."

Unfortunately, many people assign a mysterious, karma-like quality to this concept. If questioned, they will usually state "the universe will pay you back." Or Christians might say God will track these selfless gifts and pay you back through worldly prosperity.

It is a flawed concept and has nothing to do with Christianity. God doesn't want to balance the scales by filling your bucket in this life, nor is he looking to upgrade you in your next reincarnation! For the purpose of eternal rewards, he keeps track of things done in love and in the name of Jesus! If you do anything with the plan of getting paid back by the "universe," you waste your time.

Like so many other hard-wired concepts we drag around with us, this concept needs to be closely examined and rejected since it doesn't match biblical truth.

FALSE CONCEPT #2: GOD HELPS THOSE WHO HELP THEMSELVES

Work hard, be diligent, and God will promote, protect, and prosper you financially, right? No, this concept is subtly flawed as well. God feels concern for you and your daily needs but first wants to develop your character and turn your heart toward him. Worldly things are less than secondary. God illustrated these concepts to me through a little miracle I call:

"Be Stihl and Know That I Am God."

After I retired from my career job, I started a couple of small businesses, including an arborist company (I was the only employee). All summer I had been falling farther and farther behind. I would tell a customer I would do their job in two weeks, only to show up in a month or more. To cope with this, I decided to get up earlier, work harder, and push until I caught up. Still, it felt like no matter how hard I tried, things would go wrong, and I couldn't make any real progress. It seemed to me the number of negative things happening were beyond what would occur by chance. As the bitterness grew, I began to say to myself each time something unexpected or unlikely occurred, *What are the odds of that?* I knew I was subtly blaming God for letting it happen. Also, I was gently blaming him for not causing me to grow the business and prosper in terms of finances and business reputation. I often prayed that he would help me get over this mounting bitterness. I thought he would do it by helping me to catch up with all my work. Fortunately for me, he had other things in mind!

One day, absolutely determined to catch up a little, I rose early and went outside, only to find out a flash storm in the night had badly eroded my gravel driveway. The storm had washed out much of the gravel onto the paved county road in front of the house. I also had tree damage with broken branches. As I went into an adrenaline-ridden rush to get things done around the home front, everything that could have gone wrong went wrong. In fact, the things that happened were beyond probable and bordered on the impossible. As I fell farther and farther behind schedule and as each little thing went wrong, I asked myself the frustration-fueled question, *What are the odds of that?*

I chased around with a tractor and a chainsaw cleaning up broken branches for a while. When I finished, I put the chainsaw in the bucket of the tractor because I decided I would take it out later when I drove down to my shop. It was a new Stihl chainsaw, one I absolutely loved.

After I did a few more repairs, I thought, *I guess I had better run down to the road and start scooping up all the gravel before the County Road Department gets on my case.* So, I jumped on the tractor and raced to the front of the lot. I dropped the front of the bucket and started gently scraping the piles of gravel off the asphalt road. I had completely forgotten about my favorite chainsaw in the loader bucket!

I had only just begun to scrape the gravel when—suddenly—the tractor lurched. I looked down to see that somehow the bucket had cut through four or five inches of asphalt and ripped a large chunk (about two feet wide and four feet long) out of the road. I was shocked! This should not have happened by gently scraping along the surface of a road! Very frustrated, I mumbled again, *What are the odds of that?! Now I'm looking at a big bill from the county on top of everything else I'm dealing with today!*

I spent the next hour or so moving gravel and dirt and patching my driveway back to a semblance of relative smoothness. When I finished, I tipped my bucket all the way down and shook it to get any last dirt or gravel out of it, and then I drove to the shop. When I walked past the front of the tractor, I looked in the bucket and found a big pile of gravel still in it. I thought, *There's no way gravel could have stuck there*, so I prodded it only to find out there was sticky asphalt under the gravel layer.

I thought, *It's the piece I ripped out of the road, and it is stuck so thoroughly to the bucket it will take me a long time to clean out. I don't have time for this today!*

But, just to check, I grabbed it with both hands and gave it a jerk. Much to my surprise, the whole blob of material popped out cleanly in one piece. Under the blob I discovered a shiny, pristine chainsaw, saved from even a scratch by a four-inch blanket of asphalt! It didn't even have any tar stuck to it! God protected my chainsaw in a miraculous way by causing the right amount of asphalt to rip out and adhere to the tractor bucket in the perfect spot, wrapping around the saw to completely secure and protect it!

All my frustration and bitterness should have faded right there! But alas, bitterness doesn't go easy. My first thought was, *I am still going to have a big bill with the county for road repairs and it will probably be more than the chainsaw is worth!* I stomped into the shop and put the chainsaw away.

When I came out, much to my surprise, I noticed a county road crew nearing the hole I had made and soon they were busy fixing it! They made the repairs and moved on without a complaint (or a bill). I had never seen a repair crew working on our road before that day.

Once in a great while, you hear a voice in your head that you are pretty sure is directly from God. Right then I heard, *What are the odds of that?* I must admit I cried a little. My bitterness finally fled, and I felt like a little kid back in my country school, sitting on a wooden bench with a kind teacher towering over me.

If you think about it, how profound and timely were the simple interventions God performed that morning? I learned a lot from this simple miracle. I've listed some of those lessons below:

- God's intervention in your life is meant to develop your character and train you because he loves you!

- God will allow or even cause seemingly bad things to happen during the day to better accomplish this training.

- His plan is detailed, amazing, and flawless, and it comes from the perspective of perfect knowledge.

- God offers you the mind of Christ. He wants you to develop an eternal perspective.

- He longs to show you glimpses of what he's doing and to use these glimpses to remind you whose child you are!

- God wants you to slow down and trust him in the journey. He isn't as interested in blessing your results and filling your bucket as he is in developing and growing a relationship with you.

FALSE CONCEPT #3: GOD PROVIDES FOR YOU THROUGH WORLDLY SYSTEMS

God isn't subtly tiptoeing around worldly people and systems. He doesn't bow to them, nor is he restricted to little interventions to protect you from getting swallowed up by them. After you have worked within these systems for your entire career, you can become a little confused about who is really in control, but it is God who is in control, and he rules with an amazing sense of ironic humor as well.

About a dozen years ago God displayed his ironic humor to me through some occurrences in my life. I call the story:

"Look Who Opened the Door."

When I worked for a company in New Mexico, I dreamed someday I might have a particular vice president position. Since I was in a near entry-level job, several layers of organizational structure lay between the position and me, so the dream was a long shot. And, unfortunately, hope faded when the company leadership decided to eliminate the VP position and restructure.

They kept eliminating positions, and I eventually took a voluntary severance package and moved to another company in another state. As I went out the door, an executive vice president who had been good to me angrily said, "He's leaving after everything I have done for him! Well, he better not even think about coming back as long as I'm here!"

When I heard about his outrage, it didn't sit well with me. First off, if they wanted me to stay, they shouldn't have offered me a year's severance to quit. Secondly, he was putting himself in the place of God. If it was God's plan for me to return to the Land of Enchantment, there wasn't much a man could do about it!

So, for sixteen years I kept track of the man and the company's activities. One day I read in the *Albuquerque Journal* that he was retiring. I also knew the company had just been bought out by a larger company and was being restructured complete with new offices and leadership. So, deciding it might be the perfect time to apply for a job, I prepared a resume. I didn't know if they were hiring, but I sent the unsolicited resume to the fledgling company, requesting they consider me for a vice president position.

I didn't even know if there was a position open, or what position it might be. But I figured, if it was God's will, it would happen. I guess I shouldn't have been surprised when in a few days I received a call stating they would like to interview me immediately. Honestly, I was shocked, but I caught a plane from North Dakota and headed to the big city.

When I got to the office location, the building was all locked up as they hadn't begun operations yet. I circled the building completely, knocking on all the doors and a couple of windows. Finally, I heard the front door being unlocked and saw it open. Standing there was the very man who said I could never come back to this company! My heart sank—he was still there after all!

Later I found out he was filling in as the chairman of the board for a year until the company got back on its feet. To make a long story short, I eventually learned he remembered me but apparently didn't remember the angry statement he had made sixteen years earlier.

That day the new president of the company interviewed me and offered me a position, which I accepted. It was the very same position I once dreamed of landing but with several new responsibilities that made it even more interesting and challenging. It was truly the desire of my heart to have this job before I retired. God knew and understood. He wanted to prove himself above worldly systems and worldly people on my behalf!

Perhaps, in part, so I could share this story with you now.

Now, I would be the first to admit spotting irony has not been my strongest suit, but this one made it through my cloudy brain. It dawned on me that this very person who had once said, "You will never come back to this company as long as I am here" literally opened the door for me to return! I had tried in my earthly wisdom to avoid him for sixteen years. God showed me once again he is above the affairs of men. The power, influence, and will of man is fleeting. God will humble the proud and exalt the humble, if we trust him. God wanted me to understand he is the true door opener. When he opens doors, mere humans have no power to close them. Through eyes of faith, I came to see who really opened the door that day!

Not only does this story remind me of the power of the God we serve, but it also tells me a lot about how he likes to operate. He loves to show us he is always thinking of us, working things out for us, and demonstrating he will take care of us. He wants to give us the desires of our hearts when those desires align with his higher purpose and will for our lives. How many things did he have to guide and control over a sixteen-year period to set this scenario up? It is almost unimaginable he cares so much!

Had God not provided this outcome, would I have lost faith in him or his involvement in my daily affairs? Absolutely not! Walking by faith doesn't include being fixated on a certain outcome. Leave it in his capable hands.

He also occasionally reminds me we shouldn't take ourselves too seriously. We are just one person out of billions. He has dealt with every kind of sin and every kind of vanity. He even came to earth and spent time as a man in part so he could fully relate to everything we go through. He wants us to work out our salvation with "fear and trembling," but he doesn't want us to think of ourselves as all that important in the bigger scheme of things.

In fact, we are to think of others as more important than ourselves! Looking at life with an ironic sense of humor in light of eternity will help us achieve that way of thinking. It sounds kind of simple, but it is a rare ability in this world we live in!

FALSE CONCEPT #4: IT'S ALL ABOUT MONEY

Focus on money above all is a subtle cultural influence that you may have fallen prey to without really knowing. Typically, all decisions in the non-Christian work world are about money, in the final analysis. The leadership might give some lip service to customer service, employee satisfaction, the environment, or the community at large, but employees realize the almighty dollar rules the decision process. Decisions are based on the highest return or the lowest costs. Budgets are sacrosanct. Financial planning rules!

If you are like me, you were immersed in this kind of thinking for over half of your lifetime. By now, economic-based decision making is probably hardwired into the amazing three-pound instrument you call your brain. And it is good training if you can keep it in perspective. Financial training often separates the person or family who lives hand-to-mouth from those who don't spend beyond their means and strive to keep a reasonable nest egg.

However, your financial plan doesn't trump God's will for your life! Just because something is a good practice or a good general rule doesn't mean God won't instruct you to step out in faith and do something different. Either way, you need to be sure you are listening to his voice and walking in his will. Remember, the Christian life is a walk of faith, not a conservative approach to a solid retirement portfolio!

FALSE CONCEPT #5: MY TIME

During your career, you typically worked forty or fifty hours per week and the time after that was your own. You may have needed to draw a firm line, if your position allowed, or the work would have dominated your life. We all know the importance of work-life balance. However, if you apply this concept to the work God has called you to do, your vision becomes clouded. It makes you jealously guard "me time" and generates resentment toward anyone or anything that intrudes on it.

Speaking from experience, misapplication of this concept is a big problem for most retirees. You feel like you have put in your time, earned your gold watch, and now no one can blame you for doing as you please. Oh, you might do a few things for charity or maybe do a thing or two a week for God—if it doesn't take up too much time. I worked for a Christian charitable organization in a couple of positions and found this to be a real issue both with myself and with most other retirees. Every minute is a gift from

God, and he will judge how you invest it. There isn't "his time" and "your time" or "on-duty" and "off-duty" time.

At the same time, God knows all about the limitations of the human body and mind since he created us and walked among us for over thirty years. He won't demand more than we can give. He's a good Father, and everything he asks of you is for your betterment.

If we cling to our time as our own, we won't see the world in the full light of his presence and power. We won't ever walk fully in his will for us.

FALSE CONCEPT #6: SOCIAL HIERARCHY/ PECKING ORDER

We all dealt with a supervisory pecking order at work. Even if you didn't have a classic pyramid structure, there were still team leaders, managers, owners, etc. After retirement we will still tend to see the world through this lens. We might reject and resent the order, but, even if we do, we will still view the world in this manner.

Jesus and the apostles seemed to accept these earthly titles and gave respect to positions, even though the Kingdom of Heaven isn't about that. Socioeconomic status and non-church leadership roles matter to people on earth. Christians understand these positions are transitory and often meaningless, but we do live and operate in this world. Thus, we give respect where due and operate within the system where possible.

But we can't let the world system or the people in it cloud our vision or stop us from the mission. We show respect where due, but we don't defer to those we perceive to be socially or economically our superiors.

In contrast, we must not respond to an unfair worldly system with anger, resentment, or rebellion. Most retirees have a streak of fierce independence. We reject authority at most levels. We may be forced to accept it publicly during our working years, but our real attitude comes out upon retirement.

Within the church, we find a different scenario. Jesus gave real authority to those in church leadership positions. They must

41

give an account to God for how they deal with the flock. No doubt, the individuals in the church will also have to give an account as to how they respond to leadership! Too often Christians just move on to the next church if they don't like what the leadership tells them.

So, it is important we come to terms with any class structure assumptions ingrained after our time in the workplace. We must not bow or defer to the wealthy and powerful. God is not a respecter of the rich for the sake of their riches. On the other hand, we must not be bitter or angry towards those people who tend to treat us like underlings! Yes, I know, it is a high calling! Jesus responded with compassion to those who understood how badly they needed a physician. We should train ourselves to see the world as he sees it.

FALSE CONCEPT #7: YOU CAN'T TALK ABOUT GOD HERE

Most workplaces stifle evangelism. Over time, exposure to this atmosphere gives us the social sense that talking about religion is rude and disruptive. We will likely carry an ill-at-ease feeling (about our primary duty) into retirement.

The opposite is true! How "rude" is it to let someone slip into eternity unsaved? In truth, this social taboo was created and propagated by the devil himself to stop us from sharing our faith.

Think about it for a second. What do you think a person will do or think if you tell them about Jesus in a loving way? Will they really think you are crude and rude? If they do, maybe it's time they think through this taboo themselves.

You can witness to them from a position of rest. The battle has been won. You can do no wrong if you abide in him and let him work through you. Their eternity is worth any risk you might face from being outspoken.

This blinder must come off! It will only happen if Christ puts the lost on your heart. Pray that God will give you a heart for the lost. Rest in his ability to change your heart and mind, then step out in faith.

FINAL THOUGHTS ON SEEING CLEARLY

I could list many more types of worldly viewpoints we need to purge so we can clearly see what's in our buckets. Many of these viewpoints are philosophies about how God is working to fill our worldly buckets! Talk about a distortion of what God really wants to accomplish in our lives! So, you can see why it is so important you let the hand of Jesus take the second step to clear up your vision. He will replace the vision of "men walking like trees" or "the hazy outline of a bucket" with perfect vision if you are willing and trusting.

When Jesus saw the man born blind in John 9, the word used for "see" means to clearly see all of him or to see into his life and very soul. He was asked about who had sinned to bring him to this condition, and I imagine he was looking to ascertain that very thing. His was a powerful, clear, and probing vision!

Perhaps to a lesser degree, this is the kind of vision he wants to give us after he has extracted pride and bitterness and peeled off our cataracts!

I was recently at the optometrist, and I asked her if there were any signs of cataracts. She said, "No, but it's just a matter of time. Everyone gets them if they live long enough." My wife had them, but they replaced her lenses with acrylic ones that corrected her vision and removed the clouds simultaneously.

Jesus has your acrylic lenses ready to go! Your new vision will help you see yourself clearly in the mirror. At the same time, it will reveal the world around you in a brand-new light. He is the great physician, after all!

Well, since we have addressed the two logs in our eyes and have removed the worldly blinders and filters, it's time to take a clear-eyed look at those old buckets we have toted around all our lives!

8

How Did That Get in There?

"For in that day everyone shall cast away his idols of silver and his idols of gold, which your hands have sinfully made for you."

—Isa 31:7 (ESV)

I have written this book to believers in Christ Jesus. I assume you are actively yielding your lives to Christ and the working of the Holy Spirit and you are looking for insights into how to yield more completely. So, with this thought in mind, let's peek into our buckets. Let's hope it won't be a "peek-and-shriek" experience!

I wouldn't portray the pride, bitterness, and worldly viewpoints previously discussed as items in our old buckets. But they can keep us from seeing clearly what kind of ugly, disgusting little idols are in there. Obviously, like pride and bitterness, idolatry varies a great deal from individual to individual, and only the Holy Spirit can really help us see clearly enough to overcome the power of our own idolatry.

To make this point more clearly, let me elaborate on several things the Holy Spirit helped me focus on and deal with shortly after I retired. I eventually realized these things constituted monuments to myself. Self-worship is the most common form of idolatry in our modern world. The following examples depict some of the most common forms of self-concept-boosting monuments.

WORLDLY POSSESSIONS

Your worldly possessions are the most visible form of self-pro-motion and ungodly comparisons. These worldly possessions run the gamut from houses, cars, and businesses to personal property, recreational equipment, and clothing. The list goes on and on. Let me tackle a few of these head on.

HOUSES

Many, many Christians have fancy houses and vacation properties. Most Christian pastors, if they talk about these things at all, will say there's nothing wrong with owning such property. In my mind, such teaching misses the mark, and many pastors know better. Unfortunately, many are afraid to alienate some of their largest potential donors. Or maybe these pastors want these things for themselves.

In theory, there is nothing fundamentally wrong with own-ing upper-end property and enjoying it, if you can keep a healthy perspective on it. Unfortunately, not a lot of humans are capable of doing it! I have owned what I considered an expensive, upper-end home, and I have also owned much older and smaller homes. In fact, over the years, I have owned eighteen homes in nine cities in four different states. So, I do have a little experience in this area.

In fact, the first thing most people think about when they compare buckets is, *What is your house like?* Most people accept this comparison without thinking about it. If you are a bucket-car-rying Christian, you know it well yourself. You may suppress overt comparisons like this in your own mind, but you will find them just below the surface. Take the little house out of your bucket and give it a close look! When you are laid bare before the throne of God and an account of every thought, word, and deed is required of you, will it stand up?

Don't get me wrong. God owns the cattle on a thousand hills, so, the problem with spending on luxury homes is not about the money. It's not the cost of the house. It's whether the house is a monument to yourself or not. Has it become an idol? Does it showcase your wealth, your tastes, your decorating skills, or even your organizational skills?

God doesn't necessarily want you to sell the house and give the money to the poor (but he might). He wants you to deal with what your house stands for in your heart and mind.

God may want you to keep the house and use it for his glory. A large house can be useful for home Bible studies, for providing temporary housing for missionaries, for helping those in need, or for getting the family together for the holidays. Or it might be an investment strategy as well.

My parents were careful to teach me a house is just a roof over my head. It keeps me warm and dry. I try to remember to be thankful and to keep things in perspective.

VEHICLES AND RECREATION

For guys, particularly those at retirement age, these things can be an even bigger idolatrous trap than a house. The same reasoning applies to these. We need to look at each thing and let God guide us. Do we use our fishing boat, camper, or four-wheeler as a ministry tool to reach out to others, or is it a monument to our retirement? Do we take the family out to grow together in godly love, or are we trying to convince even our families we are wealthy and have our act together? Do we golf because we love the outdoors and enjoy the exercise, or is it because all the cool kids are golfers?

God does want us to take time to relax and enjoy his creation. He also wants us to stay active and involved with other people. But, when we feel like we have something to prove to others, we are still looking in our buckets.

Again, I ask: what do you do with your boat, your camper, or your golfing outings? Do you take lots of pictures and then post them on social media so your friends can see how full your bucket is, or do you use these things as tools to quietly work for God's glory? Only you can be the judge, but it takes a careful, clear-eyed examination of your bucket.

TRAVEL

Showcasing travel, adventure, and experiences can be a soft brag about our bank accounts, our leisure time, and our worldly knowledge. On the other hand, we may want to inspire others to travel more and experience the wonders of God's creation.

Once again, God can keep your vision clear and help you examine your true motivation. If you are using your travel experiences to help and inspire others, you will know it. If you are using them to glorify yourself, the Holy Spirit will point it out to you as well.

EDUCATION

I was the first in my immediate family to earn a college degree. At any time in life, a person's level of education can be something that generates pride.

I have spent some time around people I personally call "academics" or "intellectuals." Some of these folks are so proud of their education and verbal abilities that when they feel it is time to speak, they clear their throats, add resonance to their voices, and then with great gravity and self-importance prognosticate at length on a subject.

I used to think I despised this because they were so proud and arrogant! The truth is, I despised it because I was proud of my own education! I am an engineer by training, and throughout my adult life I have valued clear, concise, and to-the-point information. I felt justified in telling myself I could say in one sentence what these windbags took five minutes to say (but they got all the adulation and attention)! So, my pride made me look down on others for what I judged to be their prideful behavior.

Convoluted, isn't it!

Do you get my point? Only the Holy Spirit can guide us through these deep, personal issues and convictions and show us what's wrong in our own hearts. And, keep in mind, he isn't in the business of showing us what's wrong in someone else's heart. We aren't to focus on their motivations.

With pride and/or bitterness in the way, we could never see clearly to ask God to surgically remove our educational history from our bucket! But now, when you do pull this idol out of your bucket, look it over carefully, and you will see it for what it really is. Under close examination, you might realize you were trained by flawed humans whose teachings were sprinkled with flawed concepts. Frankly, you probably remember less than ten percent of what they taught you anyway.

Compare this little bit of knowledge with God's knowledge and begin to leave comparison with other people behind. Your degree was part of God's provision for you and for your family—not some great accomplishment of yours.

Shoot, I spent about half my time in college goofing off and then praying like crazy God would help me get through the tests I barely studied for! Give the credit where it's due. If you are like me, you deserve very little!

FAMILY BACKGROUND

I come from a great family! It's a classic no-nonsense, hard-working, frontier-conquering, got-your-back family. And there are more folks in my family than you can shake a stick at!

Family can be a source of proper godly pride, because a truly great family can only come about by the guiding and preserving hand of a loving Father. There is nothing wrong with being proud of what God has done, as long as you are careful to look at it properly. But if you start comparing your family to others, you can easily begin to think of those other families in negative and derogatory terms.

It is dangerous even to judge a family as a whole, isn't it? Each person must come to terms with his or her life and follow God down a solitary path. God is not a respecter of persons. His arms are open wide to all, regardless of their family trees.

God doesn't want us to be uppity or snooty or judgmental because we think our family is more spiritual or harder working, more well respected or wealthier, or more powerful and influential.

Look this little idol over carefully now with clearer vision. You are not special because of your roots. You are not inherently good or better than your neighbor. Toss this idol out of your bucket!

I'M A SELF-MADE MAN

Now, you might think people who aren't accomplished in the eyes of the world don't have the problem of carrying idols around in their buckets. I mean, they don't have fancy houses and cars, important investments, or educational accomplishments, do they?

Actually, without the direct intervention of God, all men and women have a tendency to generate idols and then parade them around. If you are not highly educated, you probably consider your great common sense or things learned in the school of hard knocks to be more impressive than someone else's education. Or, if you have little financial resources, you might consider yourself as morally better than most people with money, whom you believe to be generally greedy, proud, and arrogant.

So, to sum it up, retirees often compare themselves with others through the lens of bitterness, pride, and preconceived ideas. Then they determine in their own minds how they are better than other people. They then put a little self-constructed idol in their buckets and carry it around with them. When things get rough, they pull it out of the bucket, polish it lovingly through the eyes of pride and bitterness, and place it back on top so they can admire it frequently. This sad method of solace is sometimes a direct response to losing the most precious part of their self-concept: their job.

9

Now Put It Down and Step Away from the Bucket!

"The one who conquers will be clothed thus in white garments, and I will never blot his name out of the book of life. I will confess his name before my Father and before his angels."

—REV 3:5 (ESV)

I could go on with many examples of idols we drag through life. These idols feed our pride, and then, in turn, our pride hinders our ability to examine our idols. I am confident if you yield to God and let him deal with any pride and bitterness issues which may linger after your years of employment, you will be able to focus on other bucket issues one at a time. As discussed, the monuments to our lifetime accomplishments need to be picked out, carefully examined, and dealt with.

Remember, God has clearly called us to be overcomers at every stage of life. We must continue to overcome throughout the retirement stage. At the end of my life, only one thing should remain in my rusty old bucket. It's a mental scrap of paper I call my "bucket list."

I'm not talking about the traditional worldly bucket list you have heard so much about. This list commemorates the sins, temptations, and impediments to service which, by God's grace and power, I have overcome. These *must* be overcome for you to be effective and productive in the Kingdom of God. You really don't have an option if you want to finish this life well and be positioned for the eternal rewards God has in store for you!

It is healthy to keep track of what God has accomplished and to mentally check these things off as God in his overcoming power enables and strengthens you. When everything is checked, frame the list and stick it in the golden bucket Jesus provides. Your rewards are in large part determined from this list!

Overcomers like you (and hopefully me) will have treasure in heaven, where rust and decay can't destroy it and where thieves can't touch it. The book of Revelation speaks time and again of the rich rewards for those who overcome.

CONTINUING TO OVERCOME

So far, I have addressed overcoming issues we have struggled with for a lifetime. However, in our later years we face new hazards and challenges to overcome as well. If you have been retired for very long, you are probably familiar with these.

I have found the primary dangers of the retirement period are stagnation and complacency. I don't see any place in the Bible where we are called upon to be complacent at any stage of life!

I heard a straight-talking preacher exhort his congregation by saying, "You are not saved to sit." Another preacher said, "Walking requires stepping, not stopping." God expects you to actively participate in the miraculous sanctification process he has already set in motion for you! During this process, he expects you to work for the Kingdom of Heaven, while he continues to work and plan for you. As long as you live, his plan for you is still in motion.

Remember, if a chicken quits developing in the egg, the egg will become rotten. It's either growing or it's decaying; there is no other option. And nothing smells worse than a rotten egg!

Oddly, the awful smell comes from compounds of sulfur. Brimstone, used in describing hell and eternal judgment in the Bible, is an old term for sulfur as well. So, stagnation and refusal to press forward in God's overcoming power because of pride, bitterness, and all the ugly little idols in our bucket, like a rotting egg, quickly begin to reek of hell's brimstone!

Don't be this slowly decaying, stagnant curmudgeon! If you have kids, they need to see you overcome! Your grandkids, if you have them, need to see the power of God working in you! Anyone God leads you to for witnessing will respond more favorably to a growing, active, and god-fearing person they can respect. If you feel stagnant, it is time for a breakthrough! With your fears quelled, doubt and shame defeated, barriers torn down, vision clearing, idols identified and actively being removed, what is God about to do in and through your yielded life?

Without this breakthrough, what does your retirement look like in five years? Will it be an endless recycling of old reruns on TV mixed with fishing, social media, and naps? (Actually, this almost sounds good to me right now.) But seriously, it is no way to end well.

With time short in this old world, you must shift from "sitting" or "stopping" to adding to the Kingdom of Heaven. If you are already adding, start multiplying! The job of growing the kingdom isn't for pastors and full-time ministers alone. Time is short, let's mobilize our lives to bear fruit in light of eternity.

If you aren't busy with the kingdom, you will have lots of time on your hands. Extra time increases the perils and pitfalls lurking in the retirement years. If you have already fallen in one of these pits, let God lift you out and teach you to overcome. You know the pitfalls as well as I do, but I will list a few with some insights:

Lust

An obvious one is pornography and lust. Younger folks might think this is more in their domain but I disagree. Many men struggle with sexual sin and temptation their entire lives. In fact, a friend of a friend who is in his nineties says he still struggles sometimes. This sin is debilitating because it is nearly impossible to effectively serve God while laboring under it.

If you struggle with lust, flee from it. Remove yourself immediately from situations which fuel the fire. Sexual addictions and behavior are so difficult to gain victory over.

The Bible directly addresses sexual purity and the dangers of sexual sin a lot, but I find one of the most helpful passages on this issue is one where the guidance is not obvious to the casual reader. Perhaps you remember the story of when Moses and the Israelites fought the armies of the Amalekites during the battle of Rephidim (Exod 17:8–16). As long as Moses held his arms up, the army of Israel prevailed, but when he became exhausted and lowered them, the Amalekites prevailed. Realizing this, Aaron and Hur came on either side of Moses and held his arms up until the Israelites prevailed and won the battle.

Now, you wouldn't initially think this has much to do with victory over sexual addiction, would you? But the Amalekites are a picture, or type, of the flesh in the Bible. So, at a deeper level, the story is saying that the battle with the flesh can be long and difficult and victory might elude you. The key is praying to and praising God in the midst of it.

Like Moses, you also should find some good friends who understand the battle and are willing to stand with you. They will help you at key points when the flesh beats you down and seems to be winning! Accountability to these friends is key in defeating an addiction this strong.

Another sobering thought comes from a pastor I listen to on the radio. He said he has seen many Christian men who failed to overcome sexual sin and God simply called them home. In the later years of his ministry, he began to warn men that if they wanted to be around for a while, they had better get their act together immediately! This judgment also ties into the Amalekite story above as their struggle was a life-and-death one as well.

Entertainment

Another issue we really struggle with is yielding to the god of entertainment. It becomes very comfortable to let your world revolve around TV, movies, sports, social media, and other entertainment. As we do so, we allow ourselves to become lazy and build up another idol. This pitfall is as difficult to defeat as sexual sin, and it affects men and women equally.

I have watched people my age and older descend into a serious, time-consuming addiction to entertainment. It may not seem so bad if you are watching relatively wholesome things like sports and decent shows and movies, but if it takes more of your time than it should, it's an idol and must be defeated.

I recently quoted Prov 1:30–31 to my granddaughter (who spends way too much time on her phone). It says, ". . . [they] would have none of my counsel and despised all my reproof, therefore they shall eat the fruit of their way, and have their fill of their own *devices*" (ESV). She said something like, "When it says devices in the Bible it doesn't refer to electronics." Smart girl . . . it's not a direct reference but the verse actually would include them. Because if our electronic devices become our idols, we will indeed eat the fruit of our ways.

Like her, I don't want to find out what eating the fruit of our ways means, exactly. Let me eat the fruit of his ways instead!

Fear

Fear is on most people's list of issues to deal with in retirement, whether they know it or not. It comes in many forms. It can show itself via a fear of public speaking or a fear of participating in a small prayer group or Bible study. Or it can be a fear of attending church at all. Or perhaps it's a fear of witnessing or mentioning the name of Jesus to others.

I used to love the TV show *Monk*. He kept a prioritized list of fears several pages long and included things like milk and granola. His fears seemed ridiculous and trivial.

In the eyes of God, our fears seem as irrational as Monk's. Remember, God gave us a fear response to protect us from real and imminent danger. But most of the things we fear are minor, unrealistic, or self-created. They certainly pale in the light of God's power and provision!

There are many, many pitfalls that could be on your personal list of things to overcome. Each item is probably harder to tackle than the last, but our God is able and willing to take you through them one at a time! By facing these issues, praying about them, and letting God work in you to overcome, you will put God back on the throne where he belongs.

Make your list and then tackle the first item. You may have to break it down into small bites and eat the elephant just a little at a time. For instance, an addiction to entertainment might start with removal of game apps from your cell phone! And don't put them back on the first time you find yourself a little bored! There are great Bible apps, sermon podcasts, and Christian books which could occupy your time while you are waiting on an appointment or riding to visit the grandkids.

Things you spend time feeding in your life get stronger and stronger. If you treat them as more important than God or they take up too much of your time, they are clearly idols. They really aren't so different from the Old Testament idols the Children of Israel were always getting tied up with.

You might say, "Oh, Baal and Moloch were way worse than a cell phone addiction. I mean, those people sacrificed their children on the horns of their altars." Well, many children are being sacrificed on the altar of a parent's cell phone addiction. It is a sad thing to watch.

I listened to a sermon from one of my favorite preachers the other day. He said idolatry is the worst sin there is, even worse than rape or murder. This got my attention! He went on to say Jesus said the greatest commandment of all is to "love the Lord your God with all your heart and with all your soul and with all your mind" (Matt 22:37 [ESV]). Idolatry breaks the greatest commandment and is therefore logically the greatest sin.

This conclusion puts the battle to overcome "little" things like an addiction to entertainment in perspective! Overcoming is not optional. We must stay faithful and continue to grow to the very end of our lives.

I think most retirees develop bad habits over time, spending more and more of their precious remaining time doing little or nothing beneficial for the Kingdom of God. Don't be one of these folks! Be a real overcomer by the power of Christ who lives in you!

I do understand it is harder to get going in the morning and harder to stay motivated during retirement. God understands all this, too. I encourage you to consider your limitations as additional things to overcome. Remember, God has already given you all the tools you need for victorious living!

I used to have a pastor who loved to point his very crooked finger at the congregation and address the issue of victorious living (I am not sure how a pastor might have broken his finger so badly . . . church softball game, maybe?). He would say when God bought you, he positioned and equipped you with everything you need for victorious living, and he will continue to guide you through the plan he has for your life. God cleansed you and has forgiven you. He replaced your broken old heart with a new one. He attributes his righteousness to you. He gives you the full armor of God. He fills you with his Spirit and cleanses you with the blood of his own son. He gives you power, peace, and joy. He has a plan and a purpose for you.

The world doesn't have any of this, and the world can do nothing to take these things away from you. In fact, they don't even understand any of it. But *we* do because we even have the mind of Christ! This means we have an entirely different view of the world, about life and its meaning!

The preacher would comment that we are so different the Bible calls us strangers in a strange land. We are like aliens on this planet! I think his favorite expression was "You are a different breed of cat." The expression is quaint but rarely used these days. It's appropriate because you and I are inherently, radically different from the world! Don't be afraid to be different and to show Christ in you to the world! In fact, people are looking for "different." They are sick of the mundane. You are divinely made for his divine purposes and are here by a divine appointment for such a time as this!

In Heb 11:13–16, talking about what is called the "hall of faith" (a list of many faithful men and women throughout the Bible), the writer says the following:

> All these people were still living by faith when they died. They did not receive the things promised; they only saw them and welcomed them from a distance, admitting that they were foreigners and strangers on earth. People who say such things show that they are looking for a country of their own. If they had been thinking of the country they had left, they would have had opportunity to return.
>
> Instead, they were longing for a better country—a heavenly one. Therefore, God is not ashamed to be called their God, for he has prepared a city for them. (NIV)

It takes great courage to follow the narrow path through a solitary gate. It can be a lonesome journey at times. Even though the way appears abandoned or overgrown, don't think for a minute that it's a dead end. All of the people listed in the hall of faith went this same route. Christ is the gate and the way is established! The same power that raised Christ from the dead guides the lonely traveler and lights his path to the city whose builder and maker are God.

Life is a journey designed to be a great adventure. The essential elements of the story and the ending are largely a mystery! Frankly, you probably won't even know why something happened after the fact. You might think you know, but the reality is likely more complicated. God truly moves in mysterious ways. We look for times when it appears God has saved us from something bad, and we rejoice in it, but oftentimes God uses something we think is bad for great good. God's plan for our life is difficult to discern. This is why the Bible says the just will live by faith! Living by faith is not an option! If you are saved, you must live by faith. There is no alternative.

Some might say I am advocating salvation by works. But living by faith is not a work which brings salvation. It's what you *must* do *if* you are saved. The evidence of an active walk of faith is obedience to his will and his Word. If you are sitting around living on your retirement income and watching reruns on TV while the world around you is going up in flames (and your neighbor is going down to the flames of hell), then you are probably not living by faith. It doesn't mean you have lost your salvation, but it is time to begin to overcome and learn some obedience.

Living by faith overcomes fear! You can't live by faith while cowering in your basement. Living by faith must include a willingness to sacrifice. This willingness to sacrifice includes offering up everything you hold dear: your health, your wealth, and even your free time. But you can't lose in this deal, if you think about it. You are offering it up to a just and all-knowing God who will take note of every sacrifice and will keep track of it for eternal-rewards purposes. The Bible says it is wise to give up the things you can't keep in exchange for things you can never lose!

Come with me on this journey as we step out of our basements and face life with renewed purpose and conviction! We can do it with God's help and with a view of eternity similar to Christ's when he carried our sins. Looking forward to "the joy that was set before him, [he] endured the cross" (Heb 12:2 [ESV])!

10

What Does the Bible Really Say about Retirement?

"The righteous flourish like the palm tree and grow like a cedar in Lebanon. They are planted in the house of the Lord; they flourish in the courts of our God. They still bear fruit in old age; they are ever full of sap and green."

—Ps 92:12–14 (ESV)

I have read commentators who remark that the Bible says little or nothing about retirement. They conclude it's not really a biblical concept. I agree the worldly view of retirement doesn't match anything I find in the Bible, but the Bible does give a lot of pertinent guidance and a slew of lessons related to this period of life.

First, remember the Levites? They were a tribe of Israel that God selected specifically as full-time priests and servants to him and the rest of the children of Israel. They were a specific subgrouping of Israel with specific tasks and duties. Likewise, Christians today are selected and set apart for service. We are called priests, and Jesus himself is our High Priest. So, we ought to listen to God's direction to these Levites regarding retirement.

In the book of Numbers, chapter 4, God says to number those men from age thirty to age fifty to serve to carry the weight of the components of the tabernacle throughout the wilderness. In other words, if you were a Levite over the age of fifty, you were excused from the job! If you read the description of the tabernacle, you can see why God granted this kindness. The tabernacle had a lot of heavy wood and layers and layers of skins, not to mention gold and silver. Carting these items around a rugged wilderness for forty years had to be rough work! And God knew the wear and tear these physical duties would generate in an older body.

I imagine there was plenty of other valuable work available for the older, more experienced Levites to tackle. They were likely valued and respected by the younger Levites for their past work, their knowledge, and even their leadership skills.

While not providing a mandate to us, excusing the older generation of Levite from the difficult manual labor shows God's mercy towards those who have jobs which cause a lot of wear and tear on their bodies and minds over the long haul. He doesn't expect us to grind ourselves into the ground and is willing to provide other valuable work for us to do.

In fact, it was God's direction to the Levites which convinced me to leave my high-stress position and "retire" at age fifty. I didn't think I was commanded to retire or anything. I just felt like God was showing me he didn't expect me to do the heavy lifting forever. Some of the burden could be borne by others for the duration, and I shouldn't feel guilty about it.

Another passage involving age is more indirect but still pertinent in my mind. In Lev 27, considerable time is spent valuing males and females of various ages who are vowed to the Lord. A huge drop off in their value occurs at age sixty. In fact, a five-year-old was considered to be worth more than a sixty-year-old!

This valuation is a practical reflection of their remaining ability to do work versus the cost of providing for their basic needs. Of course, slaves were usually not valued for their experience or leadership abilities, just their raw work output. In my mind, it shows God expects lower physical output from his older servants.

God understands our limitations. We have good days and bad days in terms of health and energy. He is not a harsh master but an understanding God—a God who strengthens and sustains us when we need it most!

11

Parallels in Scripture

"The secret of the Lord is with those who fear Him; and he will show them His covenant."

—Ps 25:14 (NKJV)

Now, let me delve into an area I think has been largely untapped by other writers. You might have to stretch a little to agree with my conclusions. But after thinking about it for some time, I have become convinced they are on target.

Let's begin with a discussion about God's words regarding the lifespan of mankind. In Gen 6:3, it is written, "Then the Lord said, 'My Spirit shall not abide in man forever, for he is flesh: his days shall be 120 years'" (ESV).

God was frustrated with man and his sinful nature. He was sick of watching his image bearers act like animals, and he didn't want to fight and strive with the heart of man for an extended period of time. I believe God was setting a rough limit on the future lifespan of man.

People might argue the text doesn't indicate a limit because it didn't happen immediately. They would also argue once in a great while someone lives past 120. Those arguments don't deflate my interpretation. I believe he was saying he was going to shorten the lifespan of mankind to a rough maximum of 120 years.

I am no geneticist, but I have read of the Hayflick limit which essentially states telomeres within chromosomes shorten each time the cell replicates. They continue to shorten until they reach a critical length and can no longer replicate or function properly. This sets a theoretical limit for human life at around fifty replications: approximately 120 years.

Cancer cells, interestingly, don't have this limitation. They produce an enzyme which keeps the DNA data from being corrupted in this manner. Perhaps pre-flood man also produced this enzyme or something like it, since many of them lived for many centuries.

Another reference to the lifespan of mankind is found in Ps 90:10, which says, "The years of our lives are seventy, or even by reason of strength eighty; yet their span is but toil and trouble; they are soon gone, and we fly away" (ESV). This verse is merely stating what was obvious to the writer: the average Joe or Jill at the time could expect to live around seventy years. Even given modern medicine in use in most places around the world, this is still approximately true as the average worldwide lifespan today is around seventy-two years for both sexes combined.

So, after the initial long-lived pre-flood civilization and after the patriarchal transitional period, life spans stabilized at around 70 years on average and approximately 120 years maximum. God set these numbers at his own discretion and for his own reasons.

Of great interest to me in these observations is the number seventy! Now, I am not a numerologist, and I believe the study of numbers is greatly overblown. Preachers will say this number in the Bible means this, and that number means that, to make a point. Unless the Bible states a particular meaning clearly or makes it obvious by repetition, we can easily get carried away with the meaning of numbers.

But an exception to my healthy skepticism lies with the number seven. It appears repeatedly throughout the Old and New Testaments. In fact, when combined with "sevenfold" and "seventh," the total number of biblical references to the number seven is 860! It is considered the number of completeness and perfection.

Its use is first noted when God created the earth in six days and rested on the seventh. In fact, the word "created" is used seven times in Gen 1 and 2 to describe his creative work. As a result of this creative time schedule, there are seven days in a week, and the Sabbath is on the seventh day.

The use of "seven" continues throughout the Bible. The ancient Hebrew calendar included seven Holy Days which were completed in the seventh month of each year. In Hebrews there are seven titles used for Christ. In Matt 13, Jesus shares seven parables. In the book of Revelation, there are seven churches, seven angels to these churches, seven seals, seven trumpets, seven thunders, and seven last plagues. I could go on and on.

Oftentimes, seventy is used in the same manner as seven. It is also a number signifying completeness and perfection. Seventy elders were appointed by Moses. Ancient Israel spent seventy years in Babylon. In the New Testament, when Jesus was asked by Peter if he should forgive his brother seven times, Jesus replied, "Not . . . up to seven times, but up to seventy times seven" (Matt 18:22 [NKJV]).

So, seven and seventy appear to be similar in spiritual meaning. I do suspect seven and seventy are tied more thoroughly into God's prophetic timeline than we can imagine. I suspect there are amazing meanings and awesome correlations between one series of seven events and another broader series of events. In fact, I wouldn't be surprised to find out someday that the number seven is somehow tied into the design of the universe or even the very nature of God (another discussion which is way over my pay grade).

For example, many Bible scholars have said the seven days of creation correlate to seven thousand years of earth's history. At this time, it is believed by many of us who take Genesis literally that the earth is approximately six thousand years old. If this theory is true, it may well be the last one thousand years will be during the Millennium. This would place the time of Christ's return as, well . . . anytime now! This theory makes sense because the Millennium will be a time of rest for the earth and its residents as war and conflict will be forgotten for a period, just as the seventh day of creation was a day of rest for God. A supporting verse for this might be 2 Pet 3:8, where it says, "But do not overlook this one fact, beloved, that with the Lord one day is as a thousand years, and a thousand years as one day" (ESV).

Now, if you buy into this theory, don't go off the deep end and think you can calculate the exact date of Christ's return. Alas, there are several problems involved in determining the exact age of the Earth, and they cannot be fully resolved by us poor humans. All this being said, I will concede the correlation between the seven days of creation and seven millennia of earth's history as not fully resolvable, but I do lean towards its being true.

Another example of a set of seven possibly referring to a broader concept is the seven churches in Revelation. Many people believe that, in addition to being real churches at the time with real issues which needed resolving, each of these churches (with their seven candles, stars, and angels) correlates to a specific period of church history. These periods begin at the time of the apostles and extend until the church of today. I think this concept is likely true as well.

The seven annual feasts and festivals God instructed Israel to celebrate were certainly tied to significant future events. In fact, the Hebrew word which is translated as "feasts or festivals" can also be translated as "rehearsals." These rehearsals point to the unfolding of messianic prophecy. In other words, they are a shadow of things to come, the reality of which is the Messiah. The spring festivals have already been fulfilled. The fall festival fulfillments are reserved for the very last days before the triumphant return of the Messiah.

Not only do these festivals symbolize these events, but they also correlate to them on the calendar. God went to a lot of trouble to stage seven rehearsals, instruct his people to observe them, and then tie them all to actual future events.

Considering all the thought and planning which went into the use of seven and seventy throughout history, I don't think he takes the number seven lightly. Do you? I don't think any of these correlations to seven or seventy are a coincidence. So, let me pose the question to you: do you think it is a coincidence God shortened human life spans from nearly one thousand years down to approximately seventy and then noted it in his word?

For those of us who are willing to receive them, there are some life lessons to be learned from God's selection of seventy years for our lifespan!

So, yes, I went through all of the examples of sevens simply to show we can gain insights into the seventy years of our lives by studying other time periods of seven or seventy in the Bible. But it was important to set the stage. I wanted to remind you God doesn't do anything by accident. I don't believe he ever uses the number seven or seventy without significant meaning. So, he didn't pick seventy years as our average lifespan at random.

I wouldn't apply my conclusions in an adamant fashion since the Bible doesn't clearly state the meaning of the seventy-year lifespan. But I would ask you to examine the upcoming concepts with an open mind and receptive heart, looking to apply every biblical lesson.

12

Why Seventy Years Is Significant

"The words of the Lord are pure words; as silver tried in a furnace on the earth, refined seven times."

—Ps 12:6 (NASB)

So, let's begin to look at other important time periods of seven or seventy in the Bible and see what we can garner about our retirement years.

Beginning at the beginning, the seven days of creation are probably the most important to our investigation. So, I will touch on an examination of those days here, then jump to other correlations to finish the point. Then we will come back to the days of creation later for additional emphasis.

As we do this, we must keep in mind one can easily stretch types, shadows, and correlations too far. They are not meant for exhaustive point by point comparisons, just the big picture. Thus, we can say Enoch is a type of the modern-day church which is raptured before the judgment. We can say, "[He] walked with God, and was not, for God took him" (Gen 5:24 [ESV]). And this reminds us of the importance of walking with God as the judgment approaches. But we can't be adamant about a type. And we can't take every aspect of Enoch's life and try to create an application to the church from it.

So, back to the days of creation. On the seventh day, God rested from all his labors as an example to all mankind. He instructed Israel to keep the Sabbath and refrain from work activities where possible.

You can make a rough correlation of the days of creation to the life of a human as well. "Let there be light," for instance, is what happens to a baby when he or she is born. As we grow in knowledge and experience, it is somewhat like God creating more complex and higher-level creatures with each passing day. On the sixth day, when he created humans (male and female) in his own image, they weren't babies. They were mature specimens, made in God's image. They knew God and walked with God. They were provisioned and prepared to enter the next day, which was God's day of rest for him and for them.

If you buy into this as a potential type, the seventh day of creation, the day of rest for God and man, would then correlate to the period in a human's life from age sixty to seventy, as it is the seventh decade of life. If you think I am jumping to this conclusion, please bear with me as we discuss it further. For those who immediately embrace the concept because they like the idea of being lazy and not having to work after age sixty, we are not on the same page!

Others might conclude I am being legalistic. After all, Sabbath restrictions were a large part of the rules imposed on Israel by their spiritual leaders. Regarding this, I believe the Sabbath restrictions were for Israel and not for the modern church. However, I do believe what Jesus told the Jews. He said, "The Sabbath was made for man and not man for the Sabbath" (Mark 2:27 [ESV]). Based on this principle, the apostles decided keeping the Sabbath in some form is a good thing for people. The early church instructed the church everywhere they should refrain from blood and from meat offered to idols. They didn't put any of the Jewish restrictions on people because Jesus came to fulfill all the law and prophets.

However, as Jesus said, keeping the concept of a Sabbath-like rest was a good thing because it was designed by God for man and was intended to bless man with needed rest and restoration. This sounds like it correlates well to the physical needs of men and women in their seventh decade! They work hard for six days (or for sixty years), and it is time for a different approach to life in the seventh day (or seventh decade).

At this point, I hope most of you would begin to concede this point and would then wonder if there are scriptural implications for how people should conduct themselves and structure their lives during this decade or in the decades leading up to it. Well, then I suggest we go back to the Scriptures for more direction.

We all know about the Sabbath day, but did you realize God also established a Sabbath year for Israel? Leviticus 25 talks about it. The Children of Israel were to leave their land untouched. They weren't even to harvest the crops which sprung up voluntarily from last year's dropped seeds or from perennial root crops. They accomplished this by laying up extra provisions, primarily during the sixth year! So, they had to harvest and store enough to eat during the remainder of the sixth year to feed themselves during the seventh year, to plant during the eighth year, and to feed themselves during the eighth until the harvest was ready.

As a result, God had to provide them with a bumper crop every sixth year. In fact, in Lev 25:20–22, God says, "And if you say, 'What shall we eat in the seventh year, if we may not sow or gather in our crops?' I will command my blessing on you in the sixth year, so that it will produce a crop sufficient for three years" (ESV).

They were instructed to trust God for this bumper crop. But, in general, they failed miserably. In fact, when they were taken captive by Babylon for seventy years, God made it clear they had failed to honor his Sabbath years for 490 throughout their history. If you take 490 and divide by 7, the result is the 70 years of fallow they failed to observe being prescribed for the land while they were captives.

Observing the Sabbath year was a high and difficult calling, as it didn't just take faith. It also took a lot of hard work and preparation. They had to build extra storage facilities in preparation for a bumper crop. If any of you are farmers, you know how much extra work would be involved if your crop were double or triple the normal yield. And how much more work would it have been in the old days when everything was done by hand!

So, looking for correlations in our own lives, I conclude God will provide us with extra provisions as our seventh decade approaches, so we can make it through. Obviously, this takes faith in God throughout life and particularly through the sixth and seventh decades—and beyond, if you are blessed with long life. It also takes extra effort and preparation during the prime earning periods of your life.

For purposes of discussion throughout the remainder of this book, when I refer to the "Sabbath decade" or merely "the Sabbath of our lives," I am roughly talking about the portion of your life after age sixty (you know, when most senior discounts kick in).

Right about now, you are probably thinking there are some holes in this logic. Like, what happens if I live to be one hundred years old? Or maybe you are thinking you are already in your fifties and have no real means of generating extra income or savings in preparation for the rest of your life. Those are reasonable questions we will attempt to work through as we continue to explore this subject.

Another insightful incident happened to Israel when they were in the wilderness and needed provisions. God sent them a miracle called "manna." In Exodus 16 we read, "And when the dew that lay was gone up, behold, upon the face of the wilderness there lay a small round thing, as small as a hoar frost on the ground. And when the children of Israel saw it, they said one to another, it is manna; for they wist (knew) not what it was. And Moses said unto them, this is the bread which the Lord hath given you to eat" (vv 13–15 [KJV]).

God provided for them amazingly in their journey through the wilderness. He provided manna for bread and quails for meat. He kept their clothes and shoes from wearing out. He carefully taught them lesson after lesson.

The journey through the wilderness is also a vast, sweeping picture of a church-age person, saved by the blood of the lamb from a sinful life and then led and provided for by the very hand of God. The Israelites were guided personally from the land of sin and bondage (Egypt) to the promised land (Israel), a land flowing with milk and honey. However, there were hard lessons along the way. Every one of these lessons was to teach the Children of Israel something important about trusting God. At the same time, every lesson was designed to teach us in the church age something even deeper about a life guided by the Holy Spirit and about working diligently for the Kingdom of Heaven!

Manna could be gathered every day, but it had to be eaten each day. It was always just enough to meet their daily needs, but if they tried to gather extra and keep it until the next day, it bred worms and stank. However, they were instructed to gather twice as much on the sixth day so they wouldn't need to gather on the seventh day. The manna saved for the seventh day neither stank nor bred worms! On the seventh day, the manna did not appear on the surface of the wilderness.

So, what can we learn from this about retirement or *repurpose-ment*? Once again, I would make the point the seventh day is a shadow of the Sabbath of our lives. God will provide extra as needed during the time periods before we enter this time of our life to meet our future needs.

The desire to gather more than our needs prior to retirement is misplaced. And to continue to work to build a larger nest egg, instead of resting during the seventh decade of our lives (and beyond) can be a quagmire. To leave these things in God's hands takes amazing faith, faith which, like manna, comes only by the hand and through the power of God! Again, we are called upon to walk by faith. Walking by faith is the true task of the Christian. If you want to finish well, you must master walking by faith. If you need help with this, the best way to force yourself to trust is to enter a situation where you simply need God's provision, where there is no option in the flesh.

13

The Rich Young Fool

"Instruct those who are rich in this present world not to be conceited or to fix their hope on the uncertainty of riches, but on God, who richly supplies us with all things to enjoy."

—1 Tim 6:17 (NASB)

Jesus addressed gathering and storing more than our needs when he told the parable of the rich fool in Luke 12. In this parable, a man's land produced so plentifully he decided to tear down his barns and build bigger ones to store his grain and goods. "So he said, 'I will do this: I will pull down my barns and build greater, and there I will store all my crops and my goods. And I will say to my soul, "Soul, you have many goods laid up for many years; take your ease; eat, drink and be merry."' But God said to him, 'Fool! This night your soul will be required of you; then whose will those things be which you have provided?'" (vv 18–21 [NKJV])

Now, the reference to "many goods laid up for many years" tells me he wasn't just storing up for the Sabbath year. He probably wasn't storing up for what I have called the Sabbath of life, either. His motives weren't to see himself through a period when he was less able to work. His motives weren't to generate provisions for himself while he focused on a godly ministry.

No, far from it. His motives were to "take his ease, eat, drink, and be merry." There was no focus on meeting the needs of others, physically or spiritually, as it was all about himself. I would venture his additional motive was for his neighbors to see his bigger barns and for them to note his leisurely lifestyle.

Does this sound familiar to you? Doesn't it sound like most Christian retirees? Our warehouses of goods are bank balances, retirement payments, IRAs, 401Ks, and our home equities. Our eat-drink-and-be-merry lifestyles are fancy houses, boats, RVs, and lavish vacations.

Once again, I am not judging anyone for their lifestyle choices. All of this is between you and God. Your fishing boat might be exactly the ministry God wants for you to reach out to friends and family members. Your house might be the perfect place to do small group studies and offer hospitality to traveling missionaries or the needy. The RV might be the best way for you to spend quality time with family and friends over a nice campfire where you can praise God and trade stories of what he has done for each of you! I don't know, and I can't judge these things on an individual basis.

I do know, however, most people think of their retirement in much the same way as the rich fool did in the parable. They believe they themselves have laid up provisions for many years and they have every right to relax, eat, drink, and be merry. They don't see the truth of the guiding hand of God who made their land produce bountifully for a specific reason!

He wants your life to be an example of obedience and generosity. He doesn't want it to be just another parable of what not to do!

It might sound good, but the path of hoarding, relaxing, eating, and drinking is a relatively short journey full of pain and misery. Your health and your mind will suffer, and you will likely die earlier rather than later and without a whole lot of satisfaction.

God wants to give you the desires of your heart, and he knows exactly what will satisfy you. Trust me, it's not what we see on TV or read in social media!

I think often of a man who held a management position immediately before I did. It was his job to spend a month cross-training me before he entered his retirement journey. I remember he shared he was so looking forward to getting away from the pressures of work and just playing golf with his friends every day. About a year after he retired, I met him, and we spent some time chatting about life. Since we had spent so much time together, he felt like he could tell me what retirement was really like.

I remember he was so disgusted with his golf game and was sick of his friends. About all he had to say about golf was, "Getting up and going to the golf course with these guys every day is just like a job!" Later, he dropped golf all together and bought a boat, which at least he could share with his wife and grandkids. But I believe satisfaction eluded him throughout retirement. And I sincerely believe this is the rule rather than the exception.

Apart from God, work, accomplishment, knowledge, wealth, and worldly honors are nothing but vanity. Solomon called all these things "vanity of vanities, . . . all is vanity" (Eccl 1:2 [ESV]), for emphasis.

The goal of this discussion is for each of us to cast away our idols one by one, ultimately laying down our buckets altogether. On the other hand, I am not advocating we just dump our buckets over in despair. I think God wants us to carefully examine each item in the bucket to see if there is any good in it. Can we discern if these things are truly gifts from God which he wants us to use to build his kingdom, or are they actually trophies to our life's work?

If we approach this with clear eyes and an obedient, seeking heart, God will help us discern how to use (or dispose of) those things we cherish before our life is demanded of us and the things we have prepared are given to those who neither worked for them nor who understand how God faithfully provided for us.

All of this is very serious stuff! Life, death, God's will, and his provision. This is heady!

In the midst of these serious thoughts, I was reminded just a few minutes ago that God has a great sense of humor! I live in a rural area, and I sometimes burn my yard waste in an old burn barrel back behind the house. Today the wind is blowing at over twenty miles per hour, and I suddenly realized my barrel should be double checked to see if I had left any hot coals in it. As I walked towards it, I saw the barrel was already lying on its side. It was just sitting there on its side in a high wind without moving. Since the wind had been howling for about four to five hours, I wondered why it hadn't rolled across the field and ended up in the neighbor's garage or somewhere even less desirable. When I got about twenty feet from the barrel, it took off like a shot. I had to scramble like a madman to catch it and wrestle it to a sheltered location. Thankfully, the coals had been cold for many hours, and there was no danger of a fire.

Anyway, I got to thinking about why it would stay there for five hours in a high wind and then take off like someone had kicked it when I was within scrambling range. Only one answer came to me: God has a sense of humor, and he knew we would *both* get a kick out of a sixty-one-year-old man charging across the backyard in pursuit of a rusty old barrel!

14

Wrapping Up the Types

"Therefore do not let anyone judge you by what you eat or drink, or with regard to a religious festival, a New Moon celebration or a Sabbath day. These are a shadow of the things that were to come; the reality, however is found in Christ."

—Col 2:16–17, NIV

Before I summarize, let me clarify the decades I mention aren't absolute time frames. They are for general instruction and broad insights. If God wanted to give us commands, he would have been very clear. These are for edification, inspiration, and general guidance.

In conclusion on types, the sixth decade (from age fifty to sixty) is the final decade of preparation prior to the Sabbath of our lives. This is the time before retirement (or *repurpose-ment*) where we take inventory of our lives before the change of employment is initiated. We should invest whatever time it takes with God to get the pride and the bitterness out of our eyes so we can see clearly to examine the trophies we have taken and the provisions we have stored up throughout our lives.

It's a time for realistic appraisal of what our job and work history mean to our psyche and what type of impact the future loss of our job will have on us. It's a time to come to grips with whether we are still carrying a rusty, old, hole-filled bucket, or we have completed the trade for the golden bucket Jesus carried to Calvary's tree. If we still have the old bucket, it is time to carefully inspect each thing in the bucket and come to terms with keeping it or repurposing it for the Kingdom of Heaven.

In terms of types, our sixth decade is equivalent to Adam and Eve's being created mature and in a right walk with God on the sixth day of creation. It is equivalent to the double-duty picking and storage of manna on the sixth day in the wilderness, and it correlates to the extra preparation and work for the Sabbath year as given in the law of Moses.

Of course, in each of these types, God met faith in action with his consistent, reliable, all-knowing, and flawless provision by providing a bountiful harvest during the sixth day or year! In fact, the point of these lessons was to demonstrate we can trust him to provide!

You can imagine what the heathens around them said to the Jews who wanted to trust God to provide during the Sabbath year. Things like, "Are you nuts? You aren't going to plant or harvest anything next year? Well, when your kids are starving and your servants are escaping, don't come crawling to me for help!"

You can see the Sabbath year was a very high calling, and God, who knows the hearts of men, knew most of them wouldn't have the faith to actually do it. They were still carrying buckets and they just couldn't bring themselves to turn off the flow into the bucket for a year.

The Children of Israel in the wilderness were not given a choice since they had no ability to fend for themselves. God himself met all their needs, just like he did for Adam and Eve in the garden. He controlled the flow into their buckets through manna and quail, and he controlled the flow out of their buckets by keeping their garments and shoes from wearing out and by preserving their flocks. But, despite this provision and despite the lessons provided, they whined and moaned regarding their empty buckets. In fact, even though they had been raised as slaves with very little and had journeyed in the wilderness with less, God could not get them to lay their rusty buckets down. Only Caleb and Joshua did. The rest died in the wilderness, and only their descendants were allowed into the land.

It's a sad story, but another valuable picture of the Spirit-led life! The man or woman of God must die to themselves to enter the promised land of mature and productive Christian living.

We *must* lay our old bucket down and enter the land of milk and honey, and we must do so empowered by the Spirit of God and looking forward, in hope, to eternal rewards God provides and secures in a golden bucket all our own. He's working on your mansion right now! Let's quit worrying about earthly things so much!

In terms of types, the seventh decade of our lives (from ages sixty to seventy) equates to the seventh day of creation, the Sabbath day practiced according to the law of Moses, and the Sabbath year as required of the Jews. It's a time of spiritual rest. It's a time of repurposing and refocusing. Can you imagine how much time those people had on their hands letting the land just fallow for an entire year? I imagine for those who obeyed God and observed this law, it was a tremendous time of getting to know each other and refocusing on the priorities of life. I believe that like the Sabbath day, the Sabbath year was a law of God designed to bless man.

If you, like me, are in the seventh decade, time for us on this old earth is growing short. None of us know when we will take our last breath, and we may not receive a warning. My own dad was drinking coffee and playing a card game with friends when he had a massive heart attack. He was sixty-six years old and was still active and athletic. God just suddenly called him home with little warning. It could happen to me. It could happen to you. Then, your accomplishments and accumulations in life won't matter a hill of beans—they will just be something for your descendants (or the state) to deal with.

To recap and summarize a little further: just as the sixth day was a critical time period to prepare for the Sabbath, so is the sixth decade a critical time to prepare for the Sabbath of your life. And just as the Sabbath was a critical time period to prepare spiritually for the new week ahead, so is the Sabbath of your life a critical time to prepare for the next phase of your eternity.

In fact, while the Jews celebrated the Sabbath and worshiped on Saturday, the early church named the first day of the week (our Sunday) "the Lord's Day." Let the Sabbath of your life lead you rejoicing into the ultimate Lord's Day when you meet your Lord face to face! Unlike the cycle of weeks that we live in now and the twenty-four-hour periods of which they are comprised, this final Lord's Day is endless!

As a final thought, I want to say again that I am not stating these decades of our lives are absolute. I think God provided these correlations so we could learn general rules about life and the periods of life.

So, don't think I'm advocating you must do this during a time period or have to do that during another. And don't think I am saying there are clear transitions from one decade to another. I am addressing general biblical truths about the stages of our lives. Please let the Holy Spirit reveal any insights which might apply to you as you prepare for retirement and eternity to follow.

We can't be adamant about what others should do in the various periods of their lives. In the absence of definitive biblical teaching, we must not judge the behavior of others. On the other hand, I don't want you to just wave these off as interesting concepts. God provided these correlations so we can learn from them. Remember, everything that happened in the Old Testament was orchestrated by God for our enlightenment and application.

15

How Should I View the Sabbath of Life?

"And He said to them, 'The Sabbath was made for man, and not man for the Sabbath. Therefore, the Son of Man is also Lord of the Sabbath.'"

—MARK 2:27–28 (NKJV)

It's human nature to want to prove our worth. We don't want to feel old or let other people think we are. This is why we go around saying things like "sixty is the new forty." We want to show we haven't been "put out to pasture" and we still have some human capital and important contributions to make.

Many of us struggle with the desire to leave a legacy. I mean, many of us feel a desire to be important enough to be remembered for generations. We want our lives to matter. We remember our grandparents, but to our grandchildren, they are a picture in an album or a crusty old headstone. Public figures and actors from our childhood are long forgotten. Over the longer term, records are lost, governments are overthrown, land changes hands, and everything in the past seems to eventually blow away like dust. Humans fear passing unremembered into the mist of time.

Truth is, without Christ, this is inevitable no matter what we do. Nothing we accomplish in this life can grant our wish for immortality. All of your thoughts, deeds, dreams and wishes will be dust in the wind.

There is only one way to preserve your life for all eternity! You must give yourself to God and let him worry about the future! Let him guide you to him with your thoughts, dreams, memories, and (hopefully) families intact. He is so faithful and caring. He knows how many hairs are on your head!

But, striving to build a legacy so you will be remembered is a sure sign you are still carrying a bucket. If I am writing this book so my grandchildren will think of me when they read it, I am misguided. However, if we simply obey God and exemplify his truths while we live, we can leave a godly legacy which always points to him. We can be an example of what he can do through the least of us. Now this is a legacy I can get behind!

When I look in the mirror, I am a little horrified. It's not because I'm scary or particularly ugly (I hope). It's just because I look a little older every day, and I don't want people who see me to think I am becoming out of touch, low on energy, irrelevant, or—perish the thought—no fun!

This is worldly thinking, my friend, and I suffer from it just like you probably do. There are many good things about being in the Sabbath years of life, but to enjoy them fully we need to acknowledge the truth of our situation: we still have worth and contributions to make, but we don't have to prove anything.

We should be bigger-picture people, not so caught up with juggling work, kids, and tight schedules. We live with the knowledge that life is short and what we do today is critically important. We know God didn't equip and train us for a lifetime to abandon us now.

In fact, I think we, of all age groups, are best equipped to experience living in its fullness. Don't be afraid. We are indestructible until God calls us home to his throne! Let this concept sink in!

We should be like David when he faced Goliath. David had been anointed as the future king of Israel, but he hadn't yet been crowned. Therefore, he knew he couldn't be harmed by the giant or his men until he had risen to the throne. Like David, we are future kings and queens in God's service! Nothing can truly damage us if we are pursuing God's will. What fearlessness this should give us!

Probably the best part about being in this period of life is our enhanced opportunity and ability to enter the *rest* which is graciously provided by our Creator!

16

Enter His Rest

"For whoever has entered God's rest has also rested from his works as God did from his."

—Heb 4:10 (ESV)

God promised the children of Israel who survived the wilderness that they would go into Canaan and enter his rest. Oh, but you might say it wasn't much of a rest. It couldn't have been easy for the Children of Israel once the old generation passed away and they moved into the promised land. They still had giants to face and war to wage with millions of enemies!

Ah, but the learning of lessons in the wilderness is more painful than the fighting of battles once we have learned them. The real battle, after all, is with unbelief and lack of faith. Once we begin to walk by faith, the battle is no longer ours. If we have dropped our buckets, the battle is really the Lord's! Victory is assured, and it is God who fights for us as long as we trust in him.

Remember, the immature, bucket-carrying slaves from Egypt all had to die in the wilderness. They couldn't enter God's rest. Only their descendants (who represent born again, mature, committed Christians) who had learned the lessons in the wilderness and built up their faith accordingly were able to enter the promised land and experience the promised rest.

Only the mature Adam and Eve who were walking with God could enter the rest of the Sabbath on the seventh day.

Only the prepared Jews who had gathered manna on the sixth day or gathered in a triple harvest in the sixth year and who were committed to obedience and walking by faith were truly ready to experience what God prepared for them in their rest. In Hebrews chapter 3, speaking of the Exodus, we are told these Jews failed to enter their rest and died in the wilderness because of unbelief.

Hebrews 4:10–13 further explains what I'm trying to convey:

> For whoever has entered God's rest has also rested from his works as God did from his. Let us therefore strive to enter that rest, so that no one may fall by the same sort of disobedience. For the word of God is living and active, sharper than any two-edged sword, piercing to the division of soul and of spirit, of joints and of marrow, and discerning the thoughts and intentions of the heart. And no creature is hidden from his sight, but all are naked and exposed to the eyes of him to whom we must give account. (ESV)

God knows if you are really resting from your own works. He knows exactly what you are still carrying in your bucket and what you are still striving to fill it with! He also provides the Word and the Spirit which will help you see clearly. Let him show you the thoughts and intentions of your heart!

Hopefully, you have understood I am not saying the only time to enter this rest is after you turn age sixty! The passage in Hebrews is a call to introspection and self-assessment through the power of the Holy Spirit and the Word of God at all stages of life. It is also a call to rest and trust in Jesus, to walk by faith, and not to trust in works or accomplishments. Trusting fully in Jesus and walking by faith is the fulfillment of the picture painted by the Sabbath and of the picture posed by the triumphant dwelling in the land of promise.

Paul wrote in 1 Cor 10:11, "Now these things happened to them as an example, but they were written down for our instruction on whom the end of the ages has come" (ESV). In other words, "these things" happened to the Jews as an example to us, recorded and preserved as both a warning and an inspiration!

If it is essential that we walk by faith and introspection during the early stages of our Christian lives, how much more critical is it to take the same approach during the Sabbath of our lives? In some ways, it seems easier because we have more time to study and reflect and we aren't moving at such a hurried pace. But, on the other hand, it is subtly more difficult because our thought processes and mental filters are established—not to mention our hands are often a little too idle, and it is true "idle hands are the devil's workshop."

17

What Does Rest Look Like?

"Take my yoke upon you, and learn from me, for I am gentle and lowly in heart, and you will find rest for your souls."

—MATT 11:29 (ESV)

If we are to enter his rest, especially during the Sabbath of our lives, how exactly do we carry this out? I know some folks who already avoid work religiously! The Jews became enforcers of the concept of rest. In fact, they developed 39 prohibitions for each of the 39 words of the original commandment to "remember the Sabbath and keep it holy." Violating any one of these 1,521 prohibitions was punishable with the potential penalty of death.

You probably already know I am not talking about anything mandatory, forced, or "religious" in nature. Like the writer of Hebrews, my thoughts about rest again turn to the Children of Israel in the wilderness. Think about what their Sabbath was like. They sat around in tents with their children and their grandchildren munching on heavenly snacks of manna all day long. They had plenty of time to reflect on the things God had done during the week and what lessons he had been trying to teach them.

They had ample time to talk about the bitter well of Marah, for example. They likely considered whether it had something to do with how God wanted to deal with the bitterness in their hearts after four hundred years of slavery. What did the piece of wood represent? Why did God allow the water to become bitter, and what kind of a miracle would it take to change an entire well so it could supply sweet water to millions of people? Did one piece of wood change the well forever? They may have even wondered if these lessons pointed forward to the promised Messiah in some way. I imagine the questions and discussions were intriguing and thoughtful.

They no doubt discussed the law as well. Those discussions could include an endless myriad of topics. Why all the requirements for cleanliness, they might ask? Why a fourteen-day quarantine after exposure to illness or contact with the unclean (sounds like 2020)? Was compliance with the law simply an act of obedience? Or was there some health and wellness purpose behind it?

Those few in Israel who observed the Sabbath year as instructed had a whole year to do the same. The reflections and discussions which no doubt occurred were developmental and helped form children into the men and women they would someday become.

I remember when I was young and my parents would go see friends or neighbors. We would often spend most of the day and all evening "visiting." This meant the women got together in the kitchen and spoke for hours over coffee while the men got together in the living room, turned on the TV and largely ignored it while they talked about everything under the sun.

The kids would run and play, but if there were no kids my age to play with, I would sit and quietly listen to the adults for hours at a time. I would drift back and forth from the living room to the kitchen. My viewpoint became more mature, and I learned a lot about the world. Since my parents and most of their friends were Christians, I learned a lot about God as well.

Teaching the next generation is a key part of rest and the Sabbath of life. Don't give in to the urge to let your grandkids chill in front of the TV, phone, or video game when they come over. Contrary to public opinion, it is not your calling to spoil them rotten!

The Children of Israel did a surprisingly good job of preparing their children in the wilderness for entry into Canaan. Although they whined and complained enough to be beset by God's judgment and plagues, they still realized entering God's promised land and his rest could only be achieved by the next generation.

When Israel marched into the land, they were still far from perfect, but they followed their leaders and entered battle fearlessly. Having bold and fearless leaders in Joshua and Caleb (both at retirement age, by the way) helped a lot!

These same people who were groomed to enter Canaan by the training of their parents and their leaders were given clear direction to stay the course. They were to continue to teach the lessons learned in the wilderness and the law handed down by God to Moses to their own children and grandchildren. God commanded the Children of Israel to do this in Deut 11:19–21:

> You shall teach them to your children, talking of them when you are sitting in your house, and when you are walking by the way, and when you lie down, and when you rise. You shall write them on the doorposts of your house and on your gates, that your days and the days of your children may be multiplied in the land that the Lord swore to your fathers to give them, as long as the heavens are above the earth. (ESV)

We all know how it turned out for them, though. Once they were settled and secure in the land, their thoughts turned once again from doing God's will to—you guessed it—filling their buckets. Each generation seemed to teach their children less than the one before.

Not only did they fail to give the next generation the godly teaching they needed, they also offered less and less of a godly example of how to live. God interceded over and over in the history of Israel. He sent prophet, priest, judge, and king to intercede and revive. However, eventually they succumbed to worldly temptations, and the nation was invaded and conquered.

The moral of the story is living for ourselves will undermine and destroy our rest! If we continue to live only for our own pleasures in retirement, we are simply giving lip service to building the Kingdom of Heaven. As a result, we won't experience God's rest. We won't be overcomers. Therefore, we won't get away from stress like we hoped when we retired from our employment. We won't feel fulfilled, and we won't receive the true desires of our heart! And, like the Israelites, we simply won't finish well!

Pastors often have a difficult assignment when asked to preside over a funeral. They struggle to comfort the family by finding good things to say, but too often the deceased has actually failed to overcome in the Sabbath of life.

Several years ago, I heard the most requested song at funerals in the western world was "My Way," most notably sung by Frank Sinatra. I was not surprised at all. Most Christian families know this song wouldn't play well at a Christian funeral, but many times it would be more honest and appropriate. During the Sabbath of your lives, we ought to pick our own funeral songs and then live them out! Don't risk your eternal rewards and don't put your pastor in a position that compromises his integrity.

18

Abiding in God's Rest

"The Lord is my shepherd; I shall not want. He makes me lie down in green pastures. He leads me beside still waters. He restores my soul. He leads me in paths of righteousness for his name's sake."

—Ps 23:1–3 (ESV)

God gave the Children of Israel some very important and final lessons after the land was mostly conquered. These are instructions which serve us well when we try to abide in God's rest.

First, God established a system of worship. He specified where and how he was to be worshiped. Of course, we are not required to travel to the temple anymore (it doesn't even exist) or offer bulls and lambs as sacrifices. Those all pointed forward to Jesus, the Lamb of God. However, we are still called to communal worship. We are still told to respect and follow church leadership and yield to its discipline.

Frankly, having been raised as a strong, independent American, I have often struggled with these concepts. Like many others, my approach to church at one time was if I didn't agree with the church or didn't like something about it, I could find another church down the street.

However, we are called to find a church, participate, and establish some roots. One of my favorite verses on this subject is 1 Pet 2:5: "You yourselves like living stones are being built up as a spiritual house, to be a holy priesthood, to offer spiritual sacrifices acceptable to God through Jesus Christ" (ESV).

Living stones: what a novel concept! What does Peter even mean by this? Well, for one thing, living things grow. Living stones would be ideal for building a spiritual house. The master builder wouldn't have to fit each stone perfectly and then add grout between to artificially hold them in place. He could just stack them up and then let them grow together, filling up voids and adhering to each other. What a concept! The church should be like this. God brings us together, and we support, encourage, and help others to grow together into the structure he has planned!

Jesus Christ is the cornerstone of this building. The prophets, apostles, and early church leaders are the rest of the foundation. We are the top layer of a building growing through time.

One of the best illustrations of how God builds his house is when the Children of Israel, under the leadership of Ezra and Nehemiah, rebuilt the walls of Jerusalem and the temple. They worked in groups, usually formed by tribe or family group. Each group focused on a section of wall. They had to have a master plan and a master builder to ensure some basic uniformity between wall sections as they came together, but each group was responsible for their section of wall. Famously, they worked with a trowel in one hand and a sword in the other since they were often under threat of attack from those in the world around them who didn't want to see it built.

These groups of Israelites are like the true churches of today. They abide under their local leadership like the family groups, but they have specifications (the Bible), plans and quality control (the Holy Spirit), and an established foundation (apostles and prophets). Any true church must align with this foundation and rest on the strength of the original cornerstone. They are all built up together into one spiritual structure.

Unfortunately, those trying to stop the work are not just worldly enemies. They are often false churches led by false teachers and apostles. They are trying to tear down the walls. Or, if not successful, they resort to building their own strongholds just outside the walls of the church.

These imposters work hard to confuse the true church and the world as to where the church walls stop and the enemy's stronghold begins. And of course, the church can be tempted to build horizontally: to propose a compromise and reach out to the nearby strongholds, tying the structures together. But remember, we can build no other structure than what is laid out. Horizontal building efforts lack the true foundation of the church!

To the retiree, the conflicts with the world outside the church and with false doctrines inside the church can create a stressful environment. It's not a world most retirees were thinking of when they were counting down the final days of their employment. As a result, we feel justified in reducing our involvement in the church. We say, "Let the young people deal with this stuff. I just don't have the time or energy anymore." The reality is we don't want to run the risk of losing an argument or being made to look foolish. I struggle with this. It is largely an issue of pride. I spent a lifetime building a reputation and a circle of friends. I don't want my reputation tarnished or my circle fractured by being overly adamant on an issue. So, I tend to avoid risk.

Such avoidance is just another case of hiding in the basement and watching reruns instead of living up to our calling. It's taking the easy path when we are called to so much more! During retirement, our availability, experience, wisdom, and teaching abilities are more valuable than ever. Whether they know it or not, the world is desperate for what we have to offer!

BE A PHINEHAS!

Phinehas, the great-grandson of Aaron, is a rarely mentioned character in the Bible. I think of him often, however (partly because I have a grandson by this name). He is known for his great zeal for God and the law of Moses.

After the Children of Israel had conquered Canaan and Joshua had given his farewell speech, the tribes of Reuben, Gad, and the half-tribe of Manasseh asked if they could return to the land they requested on the East side of the Jordan. In Josh 22, Joshua responds:

> . . . "You have kept all that Moses the servant of the Lord commanded you and have obeyed my voice in all that I have commanded you. You have not forsaken your brothers these many days, down to this day, but have been careful to keep the charge of the Lord your God.
> "And now the Lord your God has given rest to your brothers, as he promised them. Therefore, turn and go to your tents in the land where your possession lies, which Moses the servant of the Lord gave you on the other side of the Jordan. Only be very careful to observe the commandment and the law that Moses the servant of the Lord commanded you, to love the Lord your God, and to walk in all his ways and to keep his commandments and to cling to him and serve him with all your heart and with all your soul." (vv 2–5 [ESV])

The three tribes departed, and when they reached the border near the Jordan, they built a large altar before crossing the river. This altar initially seemed a minor detail, but the reaction from the other tribes of Israel when they found out about the altar surprised me. Joshua 22:12 states, "And when the people of Israel heard of it, the whole assembly of the people of Israel gathered at Shiloh to make war against them" (ESV). Then they selected ten chiefs and sent them with Phinehas, the son of Eleazar the priest, to inquire after the eastern tribes.

When Reuben, Gad, and Manasseh saw the delegation was led by Phinehas, I am sure they were suddenly very attentive and concerned. They knew of his zeal and quick actions in putting down a past rebellion. When Phinehas confronted them, they quickly explained the altar was not an alternative place to worship God, in defiance of his law, but a marker designed to remind them of their brotherhood with the tribes on the other side of the river. Phinehas received their assurances, and we read in Joshua that when the Children of Israel ". . . heard the words that the people of Reuben and the people of Gad and the people of Manasseh spoke, it was good in their eyes . . . The people of Israel blessed God and spoke no more of making war against them" (Josh 22:30, 33 [ESV]).

When I first read this section, I marveled because I had never heard it before. I wondered what message it might represent to individual Christians and the church of today (considering all these things happened as an example to us).

Then it struck me. When we have conquered the land and have entered our rest, we must patrol the border of our lives and look for signs of rebellion or idolatry both in our own lives and in the local church we attend.

So, we retirees need to avoid picking up our old buckets again. We need to watch for idols popping up in our lives. We also need to avoid going off on our own and acting as if we don't need the church and defying the orders of God to congregate.

In the church, we who are in the Sabbath of our lives, walking by faith and resting in Christ, need to be on the lookout for false doctrines and bad teachings. If we suspect they are cropping up on our borders, they should be addressed quickly and firmly but with brotherly love.

Now, whether Phinehas and company thought it was actually a good idea to build a marker on the border, we really don't know. I suspect they didn't like it and thought it was a little presumptuous of the three tribes to do it without God's direction.

However, I think Phinehas properly decided to "make the main thing the main thing" and to leave his brothers with a sense of love and honor. Likewise, sometimes we struggle to know when battle should be engaged. The Holy Spirit will guide us in this if, like Phinehas, we approach the issue with fearlessness and zeal for the Word balanced with love for our true brothers and sisters.

Also, we should note that Phinehas didn't operate as a vigilante in dealing with the possible rebellion. He acted within a given structure and order. The authority of the ten tribes was represented by their princes which accompanied him. Similarly, we are given instructions in the New Testament for properly dealing with a brother or sister who is in sin or in error.

The concept of being a "watchman on the wall," which comes from the book of Ezekiel, exemplifies something retirees should work at. I have served on various church boards over the years. If God calls any group to be watchmen on the wall, it is the church elders! I love the feeling of unity and brotherly love I have noticed in these groups, but often they need to have a little more zeal for safeguarding the walls during construction! Do it in a balanced and loving method; be a Phinehas!

19

Radical Rest!

"Do not be conformed to this world, but be transformed by the renewal of your mind, that by testing you may discern what is the will of God, what is good and acceptable and perfect."

—ROM 12:2 (ESV)

What is radical about rest, you might ask? Well, I think biblical rest is the most radical thing a person can do! It is totally alien to a non-Christian worldview.

If you are resting in Jesus Christ, you aren't striving for your own benefit. You aren't carrying a heavy, nasty old bucket around with you. You aren't admiring its contents. You aren't polishing and presenting your trophies and accomplishments before men. You have a golden bucket, but what's in it is up to God. At the judgment seat of Christ, our actions in this life will be tried as if by fire, and rewards will be given for those actions surviving the heavenly inspection. The only way they will withstand the fire is if they were completed from a position of rest.

In fact, all these things I have urged us to do can only be accomplished from a position of rest. If we try to overcome or change our lives by striving or by sheer willpower, we will be doing nothing but strapping ourselves with additional burdens.

We will likely feel depressed and overwhelmed by our lack of progress and inadequacies. But, if every day, we simply yield our will to God and quit striving for our own petty goals and desires, we can see remarkable progress. He has amazing love for you and me and an incredible plan. Trust him for it!

Now resting certainly doesn't mean not working. God may lead you to work harder than ever, but your work will be different and much more rewarding.

Think about Noah and his family. When we think of someone at rest, Noah just doesn't spring to mind, does he? But put yourself in his place. We think things are bad today (and they are certainly getting that way), but in Noah's day evil ruled the hearts and lives of men. God said every thought of man's heart was evil continually!

Noah faced a Herculean task and nearly insurmountable odds! God ordered him to build a giant ship far from water. Can you imagine the difficulty of protecting and providing for your family while at the same time gathering materials and provisions for one of the greatest undertakings of all time?

Plus, my guess is the evil people around them didn't just idly sit by and watch them build. Satan was raging, and he likely had people mocking, sabotaging, and trying to destroy their efforts. They blamed Noah for denuding the forest, for hoarding provisions, and for building a huge, ugly, tar-covered monstrosity which would bring down everyone's property values!

Much like the Israelites in Ezra and Nehemiah's day, Noah's family probably had to work with a sword in one hand and a hammer in the other. And even though he was hard pressed to complete the job, I imagine Noah took every opportunity to preach to his neighbors about the coming judgment and the ark of safety provided by a good and gracious God.

Yet, Noah could rest assured he was in the center of God's will and had an essential role to play in his plan. His mind and spirit were focused with intense purpose. Every day he had to walk by faith, one step at a time. He was committed, sold out, and at one with God's purpose. Even though he was working harder than ever in his life, to be successful, the work had to be completed from a position of rest. He had to trust God for a successful ship design, materials for construction and an adequate labor force. He had to lean on him daily to foil sabotage efforts. He trusted that God would deliver anyone (and any creature) that needed to be saved through the flood. Amazingly, he still found the time and energy to call out to those around him. He trusted God to bring in the lives to be rescued. From the proper position of rest, he threw the fishing line into the waters of humanity, but left the results to God.

It is interesting that Noah was six hundred years old when the flood started. He had lived through six centuries and was entering his Sabbath century when the waters came! That Sabbath century would see him through the end of one world and to the beginning of another. This timing is just another illustration that God doesn't do anything by accident.

Like Noah, God wants us all to be fishers of men regardless of our circumstances. Oh, and I hate to say this, but it means dealing with people (gasp)!

I am actually talking primarily to myself here as I sometimes think I am a natural hermit! You see, I was raised on a little farm about twelve miles from the nearest town. We were so far from civilization we had to walk a half a mile down a little dirt road just to get the mail. I spent my elementary years in a two-room country schoolhouse. I still live out of town, and part of me would love nothing better than to avoid contact with people whenever possible.

People are just so messy. They have all these crazy ideas, strange motivations, and diverse opinions on everything. I would be perfectly happy living like an old cowboy or miner who just goes to town once a month for beans and bacon! I could just send money to charities to help them with their evangelistic efforts while I hang out and do my own thing.

Alas, I know God isn't happy with this approach. Ultimately, I wouldn't be happy with it either. I would grow bitter and angry with myself for not resting in God and seeking his face and his will for my life.

Like Noah, we could be the final generation before a massive judgment on the earth. How should we be living in the light of such knowledge? If Noah had squandered his time and resources, lost sight of the goal, or given up on his walk of faith, picking up his own bucket like the rest of humanity, where would we be now?

There is a generation coming soon (or is already here) which will see the rapture of the church. Will they know the significance? Will they recognize when God fulfills his prophecies, or will they believe the lies of Satan and his worldly minions? Like Noah, we have a responsibility to prepare our children and grandchildren and stand up for truth before the rest of the world.

We can only fulfill this responsibility from a position of rest!

Some Christians think they can hide in their man-made arks and wait for the rapture, building bunkers and stock-piling ammunition and supplies. But Noah and his family couldn't have been more obvious and in the open about doing God's will. In the midst of heathen decadence, anarchy, and rampant sin, they stood toe-to-toe with the evil forces and bravely completed God's work from a position of resting in God's protection. They didn't build bunkers and hoard weapons for use in driving away those who wanted to join them. They freely offered what they had to all who would come. Unfortunately, no one did.

I recently read about Hudson Taylor, the great missionary to China, who spent his life learning what rest was all about. He first learned to trust God for his own provision. Then he learned to trust him for his own protection. Through trials and tears, he learned to trust him for protection for his family and for the missionaries who worked under him. Lastly, he found out he had to put his own spiritual journey and maturity completely in God's hands. He quit striving to read his Bible, pray, avoid sin, etc., and gave it all to God.

Abiding in God's presence and trusting him for all aspects of life was a breakthrough. So, spending half the night reading and praying was no longer a symptom of a harsh, structured, and disciplined life. Instead, he simply let God wake him up and direct his heart through the day (and night). Gone was the burden of work and leadership; it was replaced by fulfillment and love. His selfless example of a fully yielded life helped fuel a great movement in China and beyond.

Most of us feel far from the maturity level of a Hudson Taylor. But his example is helpful in seeing how God wants us to rest in him. Rest is the highest calling in a Christian life and something a mature believer should be getting pretty good at!

20

Remaining Questions

"...Who have been upheld by me from birth, who have been carried
from the womb: even to your old age, I am he, and even to gray hairs I will
carry you! I have made, and I will bear; even I will carry and deliver you."

—Isa 46:3–4 (ESV)

WHAT IF I LIVE TO BE ONE HUNDRED YEARS OLD?

I brought up this question earlier and promised to address it before I finished. First, you have to decide whether you believe God
is in charge of how long you live. He already knows exactly when
and how you will die. You can't add a single day by worry, fretting,
or even planning.

Second, our job is to take reasonable precautions and lay out
reasonable plans, letting God do the rest. Remember, he provided
for the Children of Israel on each Sabbath day in the wilderness
and throughout each Sabbath year later in Israel. Technically, this
is his job. Trusting in his provision is our job. In a psalm reminding Israel of God's faithfulness, David wrote, "I have been young,

and now am old, yet I have not seen the righteous forsaken or his children begging for bread" (37:25 [ESV]).

In general, God doesn't want you to work like crazy until you are ninety so you can save enough money to live until you are one hundred. For me, reasonable means to plan to live to eighty. Unless something drastic happens to the economy, I should have a little something left over for the kids if I make it this long.

If you live another twenty years beyond your plan, God will find a way to take care of things if you are trusting him for it. You may need to take reasonable precautions like having health insurance to keep these funds from being depleted before their time. If you have children and you have raised them right, they will want to assist you in some manner, should your funds be depleted. Government protections, including Social Security and Medicare, are certainly an option as well. I am not averse to taking funds from systems I paid into.

Your concern should not be about running out of money but beginning to trust in money rather than God. If you are still worried about how much is in your bucket, you need to start full circle to check yourself again for pride, bitterness, worldly philosophies, and bucket idols.

WHAT IF I AM ALREADY IN THE SABBATH OF LIFE BUT HAVE NO SAVINGS?

This is another question I mentioned earlier. The answer is the same response I have to every question like this: God is in control and you are not. If he leaves you in a position where you need to work right up until the moment you go to be with him, I trust he can provide work suitable to your physical capabilities and provide you with the type of rest we are discussing, even while you are drawing a paycheck.

Your job can provide all the opportunities to let your light shine that a retirement could provide. Trust that he wants you there and can use you right where you are.

Let him clear your vision and point out your idols. Overcome in any and all situations, and he will exalt you later. Remember, he has us go through difficulties because we have a lesson to learn. His teaching and correction show how much he cares about you.

WHAT, SPECIFICALLY, SHOULD WE BE DOING DURING OUR SABBATH OF LIFE?

What specifically can I urge the retiree to do? Well, there are no formulas when it comes to walking by faith. This Sabbath is not about works or about our own efforts. But I will offer some thoughts and ideas to those who are eager to move forward under this counsel.

1. Actively rest in him. It sounds like a classic oxymoron, but faith comes from resting, and resting comes from faith! It's not a circular argument. It's a circular reinforcement! It's a feedback loop which keeps growing with each trip around the loop. Stay filled and ready. Your gray hairs and experiences won't carry you through. You need to be plugged in every day.

2. Call out for righteousness. You have been exposed to much training in righteousness. You have probably seen revivals. You have seen our society at a much better place. Defend the holiness of God's name to all.

3. Share what God has done in your life. We each have real-life events, like the personal stories I have shared in this book, to relay. Part of Satan's strategy in the post-church world of electronically plugged-in young people is to get them so tied up in the latest thing that old, crusty stories are hard to listen to. You will have to be creative and persistent. Having a bonfire, campfire, or special event can work.

4. Without sounding like an old curmudgeon, talk about the benefits of not being plugged into electronics twenty-four

hours a day. You have seen firsthand what this does to a society as you have something to compare present society to.

5. Witness for the salvation of others. In an increasingly secular world, it is easy to withdraw from society and shrink from your opportunities to share your faith. But many people in the Sabbath of their lives finally begin to realize what other people think about them matters very little. It's a great time to be bold, but try to maintain some sensitivity as well.

6. Study your Bible. You have time, and God fully approves of time spent this way. As the church drifts away from a true and literal Bible, you are a living stone in the wall of the true church. Stand for the Word. Avoid doctrines of men. Avoid compromising with so-called science and social doctrines. Defend the Word of God!

7. Stay tied in with a church body and grounded in a certain location. Don't pull out all your roots and entanglements with your community. Snowbirding is an option for many who have difficulties with cold weather. I understand. It is possible to stay connected with two communities, but don't use this as an opportunity to participate in neither.

8. Find a ministry or start one. Start small. You are not God's gift to man because of your great knowledge, training, or leadership abilities. All talent is on loan from God. Like my grandfather liked to tell me, "Don't get the big head." You may have the ability to work with little or no compensation, a great benefit to many ministries.

9. Give. You may have already paid tithes on the money you have saved, but what about the interest you have earned? What about the money you made on the sale of your primary residence? Just because certain gains are exempt from income tax, doesn't mean God doesn't consider his abundant provision as income. We may feel tempted to reduce giving during the Sabbath of our lives, but notice how giving occurred on the Sabbath (then) or Sunday (now). You need to be walking

by faith now more than ever. Trust him to provide. Test him to provide.

10. Like Phinehas, be on guard for signs of idolatry creeping into your life. Once you have laid your bucket down, don't pick it up again.

11. Watch for enemy strongholds in your life, in your family, and in the church. In 2 Cor 10:4, Paul wrote, "For the weapons of our warfare are not carnal, but mighty through God to the pulling down of strong holds" (KJV). Non-carnal weapons are the only ones effective in the battle against enemy strongholds. Non-carnal weapons are spiritual weapons like the Word of God combined with his love.

12. Memorize the Word. Committing Scripture to memory is so important, but hardly any of us do it. Most people think they can't do it at this stage of their lives. Honestly, I have never been particularly good about it. I know a lot of the Bible in a paraphrased form, but I haven't memorized much word for word. However, those old-time preachers you remember could quote hundreds of verses. People who practice doing this can usually add verses to their repertoire all throughout their lifetimes. My mother started memorizing Scripture in her late seventies. Now she knows several entire New Testament books by heart.

13. Participate in small group studies. Your church might provide these. There are also some great organizations out there which offer small group studies combined with accountability and overall support. I participated in one of these two or three years ago, and most of the guys from the group are still dear friends of mine.

14. Lastly, I will list the one God is having me focus on now: the concept of "first fruits." In the Bible, this refers to the practice of giving to God the first of everything, whether of one's harvest, one's livestock, or even a person's first born. In my daily life, giving my first fruits means to give him the first part of everything, including the early hours of my day. Rather than

get up, turn on the TV or the phone while I sip a cup of coffee, he has asked me to give him the first part of my day. He will reward this with spiritual blessings and a closer walk which comes as the fruit of obedience.

21

Pulling It All Together

"Jesus said to her, 'I am the resurrection and the life. The one who believes in me will live, even though they die; and whoever lives by believing in me will never die. Do you believe this?'"

—JOHN 11:25–26 (NIV)

I know all of the concepts I've outlined are easy to say but constitute a lot to put together in actual practice. If you are like me, a mental picture is worth a thousand words, plus it brings emotional reinforcement to my logical process.

I enjoy the outdoors and love to work and play outside. So, my mental pictures usually involve idyllic, pre-electronics, outdoor settings. So, please picture this with me:

You are standing outside working on something diligently. Your body and mind are busy with your work and the cares of the day. At the threshold of your senses, you feel a slight cooling of the air. You notice somewhere in the back of your mind that the shadows are lengthening. Subconsciously, you know that the day is getting on and the time to complete your work is rapidly coming to an end.

You are facing the east while you work because you are expecting a dear friend who has been on a long trip to return from that direction. Suddenly, you see the elongated shadow of someone approaching from behind you, and you hear a voice calling out, saying supper is nearly ready and you must leave your work in a little while.

It should be welcome news, but, initially, the voice creates some additional stress. You have worked hard all day long, sweating in the hot sun, part of the time running on adrenaline, struggling with the frustrations you run into on a normal day. You didn't accomplish everything you envisioned. You worry about leaving certain things undone, about leaving any tools lying around. You may even wonder what others might think about you if they see what little you have accomplished.

You have a choice to make. Do you work frantically to get as much done as possible in the time you have left, or do you slow down and cherish the moments you have? With wisdom from above, you ponder your decision, taking a moment to clear your head and heart of the craziness and stress. You remember this is the best part of the day!

If you had to compare it to something, this last hour of sun is a lot like the Sabbath part of the week. It's a time to wrap up the essentials but also a time to think through the day with a clearer head. What did you do right, what did you fail to do, and what did you royally mess up? Is there something you should address or correct while it is still called "today"?

Suddenly you detect the faint smell of grass gently baked in the afternoon sun and the irresistible smell of lilacs in the little gusts and swirls of wind. Then you hear children laughing as they run outside. They have completed their chores and their lessons and are enjoying the cool of the early evening.

One of them runs up to you and asks your opinion on something. Right then you make your choice. These children don't need to see a worried, stressed, and impatient figure struggling to fill his worldly bucket with goods. They need to see a relaxed, loving leader who trusts in his Lord's provision. You answer the child's question and then the second and third questions with patience and love. You pick up a few tools and wrap up the essentials of the job. You take time to throw a ball around with the kids and then race them to the house. It seems like they always beat you there these days!

You enter the warm glow of the house. A fire is already going in the fireplace. A veritable feast awaits you. The family is all there to greet you! Even your extended family has shown up tonight. Some of these folks you haven't seen for years. Then you see your friend, the one you were looking for, is there waiting for you. It's a joyous reunion, and because of your decision earlier, you have entered it in just the right spirit. Your troubled thoughts of the day have fled. You have fought the good fight and finished well!

If you are in or approaching your retirement years, this book might be the tool the Holy Spirit uses to remind you time is nearly up. He is marking the start of your Sabbath of life and reminding you of what's truly important during this time. It's been a great journey! Take time to reflect and appreciate things while it's still called today. Choose to quit struggling on your own and really begin to rest! He has promised true joy ahead. The week is nearly up; the day is nearly over. It doesn't mean an end, just the beginning of something new and better!

In the New Testament church, the day following the Hebrew Sabbath (Saturday) is called the Lord's Day (Sunday). So, the first day of a brand-new week is called the Lord's Day. And the day he returns, and we meet him face to face is called "the Day of the Lord." I think this day will be soon, but if you are a little older like me and die (or are raptured) beforehand, it will be like our own Day of the Lord when we meet him face to face.

Make sure you prepare your heart during this Sabbath of life for the imminent Day of the Lord and your life with him! After all, the Sabbath was made for man for the very purpose of resting and growing closer to the Lord in preparation for the week ahead!

Back to the little story about working in the yard until you are called home. I portrayed entering the door to the house as being simple in the story. Some have characterized death as crossing an icy river or fighting the last war with pain or as a struggle with the Grim Reaper. Thank God that Jesus has fought the battle and won the victory over death for us. As Christians we have already entered eternal life and this life is secure in him if we stay faithful. Death isn't bitter. Death isn't an end. It's not even a beginning. It's a continuation, merely opening a door into another place. Eternal life follows physical death as seamlessly as morning follows night! It's not an icy river or a final, grim battle! We can move from the Sabbath of life right into the Day of the Lord as easily as Sunday follows Saturday because Jesus has conquered death!

Yes, we might have to endure trials and pain before the door is opened, but we need to rest in the assurance these trials serve to glorify God and showcase his love through us to those who need to see it most. God knows exactly whom we will touch in those final hours on earth, and your eternal rewards will accumulate as you obey. Jesus went through this very thing and, because he knew what joys awaited him, was obedient to die a sinner's death.

One shortcoming of the little story above is its focus on the individual. The story of our lives, and even all of history (*his*-story), is about Jesus Christ! In the story, he was just a dear friend waiting for us, but truly, he is everything to the believer.

If you overcome now, when you meet him face to face, you will certainly hear him say, "Well done, good and faithful servant . . . Enter into the joy of your master!" (Matt 25:23 [ESV]) These are words you and I should long to hear!

A friend recently said to me, "I hope I am so heavenly minded when I cross over there will be no huge shock!" He went on, "But, I expect it will be so magnificent and beyond my imagination that there will be." Obviously, the story above doesn't address this aspect of dying, either. I suppose we could be so heavenly minded on earth that heaven won't seem so different, but I don't believe I've ever met anyone quite this far in his or her relationship and walk with God.

Another friend used to comment on people who are "so heavenly minded that they are of no earthly good," but I have never actually met this kind of person, either.

It's true that seventy years of living in a three-dimensional universe on the third rock from old Sol doesn't equip you fully for transitioning to four-dimensional living with Jesus as your sole illumination. But, if we walk with the Lord, we will gain more of an eternal (or four-dimensional) perspective. If we walk in the light, as he is in the light, we will not be so shocked by his glory when we behold it fully!

22

Call to Action

"Oh come, let us sing to the Lord; let us make a joyful noise to the rock of our salvation! Let us come into his presence with thanksgiving; let us make a joyful noise to him with songs of praise! For the Lord is a great God, and a great King above all gods. In his hand are the depths of the earth; the heights of the mountains are his also. The sea is his, for he made it, and his hands formed the dry land . . ."

—Ps 95:1–11 (ESV)

"So how can I really do all this?" you might ask. "How can I move forward with real, lasting change?" There's only one way! If you have given your life to Jesus, the power that raised him from the grave lives in you! He is eager to act on your behalf to see these changes take root.

We know if we ask something according to his will, we have it. All effectual prayer starts with God. He places a desire in our heart to obey, and then we pray for his will to happen. If you feel his presence guiding you to lay down your bitterness and pride along with your worldly idols, know for certain it is his will you do so. And know for certain he will bring life-changing power and unquenchable fire to burn up the wheat and stubble in your life, leaving the gold, silver, and precious jewels behind.

If you haven't already, separate yourself from the world! Operate from a Christian base of strength with the support of praying family and/or saved brothers or sisters. Know of the world and its ways but avoid being a part of it. Don't watch its TV programs and movies. Don't listen to its music (except to sample or educate yourself). Worldly golf and fishing buddies can make this extremely difficult!

Four years ago, I hiked Kilimanjaro with five other guys. Our group included three missionaries, one missionary consultant, one atheist, and me. The hike reminded me of our walk on this earth! It stretched on and on. At times it was exciting. Other times it was more like drudgery. The Christians in the group took turns walking alongside the atheist, telling him about Christianity and witnessing to him. From my perspective, the act of witnessing built a wonderful camaraderie in the group and kept the Spirit of God working and present in a special way. I tended to forget about the pain of the journey as I focused on the lost soul near me and how God could reach him.

When I thought about it later, I realized how different it would have been if I had hiked the mountain with five atheists! They would have made the trip miserable. I may have struggled with my faith before it was over. The journey would have been frustrating, likely an emotional roller-coaster.

Life is like this. You need to surround yourself with a support group of brothers and sisters who are all focused on winning the lost souls along life's trail.

The Bible sometimes depicts the individual as afloat in the "sea of humanity." I see the non-saved as bound by three chains while they struggle to stay afloat. These chains are sin, death, and the power of the devil. The Christian has a chain as well. But he is not bound by it. Rather, this chain is his lifeline! The other end pierces the veil of heaven and is anchored on the very throne of God!

If you have nothing but worldly people on every side, they will surround you, latch on, and frantically try to drag you to the bottom with them. So, keep a support structure of Christian brothers and sisters around you as you reach out to the lost!

COME TO GRIPS WITH EVIL IN THE WORLD

While we are on the subject of the fallen people around us, I would be remiss not to address the issue of how alien present society might seem to you. The world we see before us doesn't look anything like the world we knew in the fifties, sixties, or seventies, does it? We find ourselves asking how we can make a difference in a world that has fallen so far so fast.

It all seems so chaotic, with mass confusion and growing insanity. Wrong is called right and right is called wrong. Deception is elevated above truth and no one seems concerned about any kind of judgment from God or anyone else.

I think it wise to come to grips with just how fallen the world system and popular culture truly is. Doing so helps us to focus on the three chains which bind the lost:

The first chain is sin.

They want their sin! To these people, anything standing in the way of the freedom to sin must be pulled down! Whether it's the Bible, conservative Christian values, politicians who aren't part of their support structure, the police, laws against abortion, etc. Anything impeding their sinful lifestyles or causing them to feel guilty must be ripped down at any cost.

The second chain Is death.

A culture of death ensnares many. At its most basic level, it is rejection of the sanctity of life. It is fueled by a belief in evolution and the rejection of God. This chain makes abortion a litmus test for the sinner who is voting. Taken to the frightful conclusion, it enables abortion at any stage and the execution of anyone seen by the enlightened as a drag on society.

The third chain is the power of the devil.

The devil motivates people to commit many atrocities. At its basic level, this chain causes people to resist and attack everything God has said or established as true. As an example, one of the first things God said about humans in Genesis was that he created them male and female. We know how this basic truth is now resisted in our society.

Anything and *everything* God said *must* be attacked endlessly by these people. Their master is the devil, and his will is to oppose God and to exalt himself above God in every way and at every turn. In fact, the final battle of Armageddon will apparently be in defiance of God's promise to Abraham to provide the land of Israel to the Jews as an eternal inheritance.

In addition to knowing what motivates the lost around us, we must fully realize how fallen they are and how bad their sin really is. Jesus said in Matt 18:6 that it would be better for someone to have a millstone hung around his neck and to be thrown into the sea than it would be for them to cause a believer to stumble. Wow! A millstone is worse than a chain when you are treading water in the sea of life!

In spite of this warning, the agents of the evil one push their agendas in schools, teaching children to hate and fear their classmates and neighbors. They permeate libraries, nurses' offices, and government agencies in an effort to confuse children regarding their own gender, going so far as to talk them into taking dangerous drugs and having irreversible surgery. They convince children not to confide in their parents. They teach them life-changing myths about science and evolution.

Look how fallen they are! Look how motivated they are to sin, kill, and destroy. See who their father is. Don't hate them, but know who they are. Hate what they do and what they stand for. Give their arguments no credence. Pray for them in love.

In some parts of the world, these people seem to greatly outnumber the children of God. I encourage you to come out from among them so you can operate in the type of environment I experienced climbing Kilimanjaro. However, it may not be possible given your circumstances and your family's location.

BE THE UNDERDOG IN THIS ADVENTURE

If you are outnumbered and have to play the role of the underdog, remember God loves an underdog. The Bible is full of underdogs whom God used in amazing ways!

- He turned a slave baby in Egypt into a victor over the Egyptian empire and their god-king.

- He turned a shepherd boy into a giant slayer and established his line of kings forever!

- Jesus was born in a manager in the humblest of circumstances. He lived under the thumb of one of the strongest and most ruthless empires ever. Yet, he is now seated on the very throne your anchor clings to!

The list could go on for pages. The point is life is a grand adventure God has prepared for you, and he has simultaneously prepared you for it!

Look at the horrible people, bad governments, demonic powers, and deplorable circumstances these folks experienced. Now their names are in the hall of faith we discussed before! If we examine present society in the light of the history of the world and the persecution other saints have endured, we realize that our struggles with societal change and evil in the world are not all that unique. The godly life has always been like this. This knowledge motivates me to join the good fight that God's children have always faced.

I once read about a gentleman who grew up in a family which promoted faith and Judeo-Christian teachings. Unfortunately, as he grew older, he experienced a rapidly changing world and a greatly changed culture. He was surrounded more and more by godless attitudes and rampant sin. Drunkenness and wild parties became the rule rather than the exception. The culture was inundated with coarse entertainment. People became irreverent and uneducated regarding the things of God. For the most part, they lost any understanding they may have once had about God's role in creation. They forgot about the laws of sin and death. They didn't know much about God's love or his offer of a Savior. Pride in the strength of the nation's army and the wisdom of its ruling class replaced most people's faith in God.

Despite the constant pressure from his environment, the man was faithful to God and worked diligently at his white-collar administrative job. He endured intense workplace turmoil, surviving ruthless layoffs and terminations.

At his place of employment, the office politics seemed endless and merciless. He suffered through baseless allegations and occasional setbacks as a result. His fellow employees even went so far as to persuade the boss to enact policies which directly opposed the practicing of his faith. God intervened several times on his behalf to preserve him.

Fortunately, over the years, each employer came to realize this man wasn't interested in self-promotion or office politics. Plus, he exhibited wisdom, diplomacy, and more attention to detail than his peers.

He survived a major corporate takeover where many other employees were terminated on the spot. The period after the takeover was chaotic and complicated further by a merger. But he always landed on his feet. In fact, he always seemed to rise to the highest available positions.

Through his long and varied career, God protected his heart from bitterness. Through a focus on the Word of God and daily prayer and supplication, he avoided the worldly blinders and cultural influences one would expect might blur his vision.

Although he had opportunity for great wealth, he neither developed a sense of pride nor carried a bucket filled with worldly idols. He lived simply and humbly.

As this gentleman grew older and approached retirement age, he came to understand a seventy-year time period was spelled out in the Word of God. He was focused on finishing well, and he wanted to rest more fully in God, spending more time in his Word. In doing so, he became focused on both near-term and long-term predictions as revealed by God through his angels and prophets.

He also prayed repeatedly for God to forgive his fellow countrymen for their many years of rampant disobedience to his commands and their lack of faith. He prayed for God's favor toward his people and the restoration of their nation.

As he became more in tune with God's will, he began to pray earnestly for God's plan to come to fruition soon. He became concerned with upcoming major world events and the role of his nation in them.

In addition to spiritual restoration, he prayed for things like the restoration of the nation of Israel, the building of a new temple, and the return to the earth of a new Jerusalem. He began to pray for people of like faith to be suddenly removed from the culture and taken to the promised land where they could live in peace and have a descendant of King David on the throne forever.

Even though he was getting too old to see all these events to fruition, he wanted to be involved in as much of it as possible and to influence his world in preparation for them. God honored his prayer wondrously and revealed many details of his plan to him. This man faithfully studied and strove to understand what God had revealed. He fastidiously recorded what he learned.

God used him to impact his generation, maybe like no one who had gone before.

This guy sounds like a perfect model for our generation. Like him, we find ourselves at a crossroad of major events. Time is short. Our seventy years is up or nearly up and we have little time left to influence our culture. God will cause his plan to happen regardless of what we do, but we want to play a role in it if he will use us!

Oh, in case you didn't guess: the gentleman in this story is the prophet Daniel! I may have filled in a little with some educated guesses about the man, but I do believe all the parts of the narrative are highly likely. And indeed, no study on biblical retirement would be complete without examining one of the most revered lifelong servants of God.

Daniel, like us, was a stranger in a strange land. He strove to keep himself separate from the world, avoiding its sin and decadence. He showed himself to be more diligent, better informed, and harder working than his peers during his career. But he did everything for the glory of God. He wasn't living to fill his own bucket. He wasn't influenced by his culture or contaminated by the values of the dying Babylonian Empire he served.

Just like him, we are exiles in this land. We must maintain this perspective, or we will become indistinguishable from those around us. We need to employ the mindset of just passing through as we keep our eyes set on our true home. The writer of Hebrews, speaking of the great heroes of the faith, states:

> These all died in faith, not having received the promises, but having seen them afar off were assured of them, confessing that they were strangers and pilgrims on the Earth. For those who say such things declare plainly that they seek a homeland. And truly if they had called to mind that country from which they had come out, they would have had the opportunity to return. But now they desire a better, that is, a heavenly country. Therefore, God is not ashamed to be called their God, for he has prepared a city for them. (Heb 11:13–16 [ESV])

Their exile in Babylon was decreed to be seventy years, much like our average lifespan (exile period) in this world. Those of us at or near retirement age must come to grips with the concept that the seventy years for us, like Daniel, is nearly up. It's time to enter radical rest! It's time to apply the things we learned in a lifetime of study and service.

Daniel wasn't anything special in and of himself. He was just a regular working guy whom God molded. He maintained obedience to God regardless of circumstances and exemplified a life of integrity. He was a man who kept his vision clear and carefully examined his bucket for idols. His bucket list was a checklist of temptations resisted, sins avoided, and times of total reliance on his God. He flourished spiritually as an exile, a stranger in a strange land.

Although he was originally interested in the seventy-year period and the transitions to come, God showed him so much more! Because he sought God and prayed selflessly, God sent Gabriel himself to deliver the most sweeping and detailed prophecies received by man to that point. Those prophecies included the near-term things he was looking for: things like the restoration of Israel, the building of another Jerusalem, and the reconstruction of the temple. They also pointed through time to the Messiah, his death, and even his second coming.

The ripples of this faithful servant's life and the revelations given to him will continue to surge through the sea of humanity until all is fulfilled. The life of Daniel, particularly his later days, exemplifies everything I have been talking about. He is a tremendous example to the retiree!

MOVE QUICKLY WITH PRAISE AND WORSHIP

Let's return to the concept of moving forward with lasting change in our personal transition. Another key to quick progress in your transformation is to enter his presence with praise. Spend time praising, listening, and seeking. He will instruct you in the journey. Receive his life-changing power with faith and thanksgiving.

I don't think most pastors today talk much about the power of praise or show people how to enter it. I hesitate to talk to mature Christian retirees like you about the fundamentals of praise and worship. However, since I once had such a fundamental lack of understanding, I suspect many others do as well.

There's a song (and a psalm) which says, "I will enter his gates with thanksgiving in my heart. I will enter his courts with praise. I will say this is a day that the Lord has made. I will rejoice for he has made me glad." I love this song! We tend to think of praise as something we do when we sing in church. That certainly should be praise, but if we only do it in front of others as directed by the music leader, we are a bit hypocritical! We should offer praise to God every day. Doing so is a great way to enter an awareness of his presence and tune into life-changing power which flows from the Holy Spirit into your heart and life.

The first charismatic church I attended placed a strong emphasis on praise and worship. Many people raised their hands and some praised and prayed out loud. I had come from a conservative Lutheran background and didn't know what to think about it all. But the pastor wisely guided us through Scriptures related to praise. He explained how King David and others would worship God without fear of what others thought.

I eventually became convinced it was an aspect of Christian life of which I was largely ignorant. Also, I could clearly feel God's presence in the church. Feelings of love, joy, wonder, and thanksgiving would come upon me. I knew such feelings were legitimately from God, and I wanted to know more.

The pastor suggested several ways to praise and worship on our own. I found them all effective. God's peace and joy would pour into my heart. I had never felt the Holy Spirit like that before. The Spirit gave me an intense desire to see people saved. He also provided love and fellowship with fellow Christians. He gave me power to overcome several things in my life.

I learned an essential element of praise is resting in God. The author of Hebrews wrote, ". . . for he who comes to God must believe that he is and that he is a rewarder of those who diligently seek him" (11:6 [NKJV]). So, it's not about your efforts or will when you praise him. It's not about your breakthroughs, works, or personal efforts. It's about being amazed at who he is and what he does! It's about trusting he can work out your spiritual journey (like Hudson Taylor learned). He not only knows what you need, but he is willing to provide it to you right now!

An excellent way to praise when alone is to dwell on God's attributes at length. You can repeat the names and titles God has given himself, trying to absorb the depth and meaning of each wonderful label or title: Creator, Savior, Friend, Father, Alpha and Omega, King of Kings, Lord of Lords, bright Morning Star, soon coming King, Jehovah . . . the list goes on and on.

State frequently that the God of glory is welcome in this place (your heart and soul). Why does the one who makes everything and sustains it care so much about the tiny person who goes by your name? His thoughts toward us are without end. His love is amazing. Hallelujah!

Take your time. Trust him with your sanctification and spiritual journey. Read the Bible in between praise periods. Know he wants to bless you with a closer walk and endless fellowship. Feel the joy and wonder in his presence. Say "Hallelujah" a lot! He is worthy.

I loved the old-time church services and revivals which ended with an altar call. It was a time to dwell on the message just received and bring it to focus immediately in my life. Those altar calls were effective largely because the participants knew how to enter his presence with praise. They also knew how to stop praising when appropriate and listen closely. Their hearts were soft and yielded to the Master.

Usually, I was one of the last ones to go forward. I was worried about what other people might think about me and afraid to let them see me become emotional. But every time I yielded and spent time glorifying my Lord and Savior at the altar, I was glad I had done so.

Many churches have forgotten how to praise. Or we cut it short and rush off to pursue one of our frivolous pastimes.

Praise has amazing power. God intends everything he has provided us in life to draw us into a closer relationship with him. His perfect Word draws us to praise him. The shed blood of his son draws us to praise him. His wonderful creation draws us to praise him. His plan and provision for us draw us to praise him. His concern about our eternity and our rewards draws us to praise him. God inhabits those praises. Spend time on your knees in praise and worship, and he will change your heart faster than you can imagine!

While you are praising, be sure to pray for those toward whom you feel bitter or pridefully jealous. Don't let unforgiveness hamper your prayers or the closeness of your walk with God.

As you praise, you must believe he wants to bless you with more of his presence. Enter those gates . . . wander around his courts in awe! It's where you belong. It's where you were reborn to live. This is your birthright, and it's independent of any church or doctrine. The Holy Spirit is your earnest money on the future riches of your incredible inheritance! And like Jesus when he moved and worked on this earth, the Holy Spirit can make quick work of your problems and your issues left from a lifetime of walking in a fallen world!

We might as well get used to spending time in praise. It's good practice for eternity.

The shadows are getting long. There's a slight chill in the air as the day begins to wind down. It won't be long now until the supper bell rings for you and me! True peace and joy for yourself and others is at stake! Your heavenly rewards are not fully determined! The eternal destinies of those around you are in the balance. If we are going to finish well, now is the time to get our hearts right before our God and maker. He is the perfecter of our faith!

Make the decision to create a new bucket list, and then finish this life in the best way possible: from a radical position of rest and obedience.